BIG BAD-ASS
BOOK OF
SHOTS

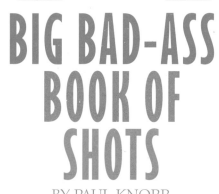

BIG BAD-ASS
BOOK OF
SHOTS

BY PAUL KNORR

RUNNING PRESS
PHILADELPHIA • LONDON

20   19   18   17   16   15
Digit on the right indicates the number of this printing

Library of Congress Control Number: 2004103056

ISBN: 978-0-7624-1901-2

Front cover design by Alicia Freile
Back cover design by Serrin Bodmer
Interior design by Bill Jones (Running Press) and NOVA Graphic Services
Edited by Lindsay Powers (Running Press) and Marta Steele (NOVA
Graphic Services)
Typography: Block BE, Bulldog, Garage Gothic, Palatino, Bodega Sans,
and Helvetica Condensed

This book may be ordered by mail from the publisher. Please include
$2.50 for postage and handling.
But try your bookstore first!

Running Press Book Publishers
2300 Chestnut Street
Philadelphia, PA 19103-4371

Visit us on the web!
www.runningpress.com
www.runningpresscooks.com

*To my wife Nicole, my daughter Camryn,
and to all the friends I've raised a glass with
over the years.*
—Paul Knorr

TABLE OF CONTENTS

A-BOMB
1 part vodka
1 part coffee liqueur
Splash of cold coffee
Shake with ice and strain into a shot glass.

ABSOHOT
1 part Absolut Peppar®
Dash of hot sauce
Pour vodka into a shot glass neat
(do not chill). Top with a dash of hot sauce.

ABSOLUT HUNTER
2 parts vodka
1 part Jägermeister®
Shake with ice and strain into a shot glass.

ABSOLUT PEPPARMINT
1 part Absolut Peppar®
Dash of peppermint schnapps
Shake with ice and strain into a shot glass.

ABSOLUT QUAALUDE
1 part Absolut® vodka
1 part Frangelico®
1 part Irish cream
Shake with ice and strain into a shot glass.

ABSOLUT ROYAL FUCK

2 parts Crown Royal® bourbon
1 part Absolut Kurant®
1 part peach schnapps
Splash of cranberry juice cocktail
Splash of pineapple juice
Shake with ice and strain into a shot glass.

ABSOLUT TESTA ROSSA

2 parts Absolut® vodka
1 part Campari®
Shake with ice and strain into a shot glass.

ABSOLUT TOOCH
1 part Absolut® vodka
1 part Southern Comfort®
1 part tequila
1 part raspberry liqueur
1 part triple sec
Splash of pineapple juice
Splash of cranberry juice cocktail
Shake with ice and strain into a shot glass.*

*Note: Because this recipe includes many ingredients,
it's easier to make in volume, about 6 shots.

ABSOLUTELY FRUITY
1 part 99-proof banana liqueur
1 part watermelon schnapps
1 part Absolut® vodka
Shake watermelon and banana alcohol with
ice and strain into a shot glass.
Top with vodka.

ABUSE MACHINE
2 parts tequila
1 part whiskey
1 part sambuca
Splash of hot sauce
Splash of Worcestershire sauce
Shake with ice and strain into a shot glass.

ACAPULCO
1 part tequila
1 part pineapple juice
1 part grapefruit juice
Shake with ice and strain into a shot glass.

ACID
1 part 151-proof rum
1 part 100-proof bourbon
Pour ingredients into a glass neat
(do not chill).

ACID COOKIE
1 part Irish cream
1 part butterscotch schnapps
1 part 100-proof cinnamon schnapps
Splash of 151-proof rum
Shake with ice and strain into a shot glass.

ADIOS MOTHERFUCKER
1 part coffee liqueur
1 part tequila
Layer in a shot glass.

ADULT LIT
1 part dry gin
1 part vodka
1 part light rum
1 part triple sec
Shake with ice and strain into a shot glass.

ADVO SHOOTS
2 parts blue curaçao
1 part advocaat
Shake with ice and strain into a shot glass.

ADVOSARY
2 parts maraschino liqueur
1 part advocaat
Layer in a shot glass.

AFFAIR SHOT
1 part strawberry schnapps
1 part orange juice
Shake with ice and strain into a shot glass.

AFTER 5
1 part coffee liqueur
1 part peppermint schnapps
1 part Irish cream
Layer in a shot glass.

AFTER DARK
1 part coffee liqueur
1 part Irish cream
1 part Licor 43®
Layer in a shot glass.

AFTER DINNER
1 part brandy
1 part cherry brandy
Dash of lemon juice
Shake with ice and strain into a shot glass.

AFTER EIGHT
1 part coffee liqueur
1 part crème de menthe
1 part Irish cream
Layer in a shot glass.

AFTERBURNER 1
1 part cinnamon schnapps
1 part 151-proof rum
Pour ingredients into a glass neat
(do not chill).

AFTERBURNER 2
2 parts vodka
1 part hot sauce
Pour ingredients into a glass neat
(do not chill).

AFTERBURNER 3

1 part pepper-flavored vodka
1 part coffee liqueur
1 part Goldschläger®
Pour ingredients into a glass neat
(do not chill).

AFTERLANCHE

1 part Aftershock® cinnamon schnapps
1 part Avalanche® peppermint schnapps
Layer in a shot glass.

AGENT 99

1 part Grand Marnier®
1 part Marie Brissard Parfait Amour®
1 part anisette
Layer in a shot glass.

AGENT ORANGE 1

1 part vodka
1 part rum
1 part gin
1 part Southern Comfort®
1 part Yukon Jack®
1 part DeKuyper® Sour Apple Pucker
1 part melon liqueur
2 parts grenadine
3 parts orange juice

Shake with ice and strain into a shot glass.*

*Note: Because this recipe includes many ingredients,
it's easier to make in volume, about 6 shots.

AGENT ORANGE 2

1 part Southern Comfort®
1 part Jack Daniel's®
Splash of orange juice

Shake with ice and strain into a shot glass.

AGGRESSIVE BLOW JOB
1 part grain alcohol
3 parts cola
Shake with ice and strain into a shot glass.

AIRHEAD
1 part peach schnapps
1 part cranberry juice cocktail
Shake with ice and strain into a shot glass.

ALABAMA SLAMMER 1
1 part Southern Comfort®
1 part amaretto
Splash of orange juice
Splash of pineapple juice
Shake with ice and strain into a shot glass.

ALABAMA SLAMMER 2

2 parts Southern Comfort®
2 parts amaretto
1 part sloe gin
Splash of lemon juice
Shake with ice and strain into a shot glass.

ALABAMA SLAMMER 3

2 parts Southern Comfort®
1 part amaretto
4 parts cranberry juice cocktail
Shake with ice and strain into a shot glass.

ALASKAN OIL SLICK
1 part blue curaçao
1 part peppermint schnapps
Splash of Jägermeister®
Shake first two ingredients with ice
and strain into a shot glass.
Top with Jägermeister®.

ALBERTAN ASSHOLE
2 parts orange juice
1 part amaretto
1 part vodka
Layer in a shot glass.

ALCUDIA

2 parts dry gin
1 part Galliano®
1 part crème de banana
1 part grapefruit juice
Shake with ice and strain into a shot glass.

ALICE FROM DALLAS SHOOTER

1 part coffee liqueur
1 part Mandarin Napoleon® liqueur
1 part tequila gold
Shake with ice and strain into a shot glass.

ALIEN

1 part blue curaçao
Splash of Irish cream
Shake blue curaçao with ice and strain into a shot glass. Slowly pour Irish cream into the center to form the "alien."

ALIEN NIPPLE

2 parts butterscotch schnapps
1 part Irish cream
1 part melon liqueur
Add butterscotch first, layer Irish cream on top, and pour melon liqueur in the center.

ALIEN SECRETION
1 part vodka
1 part melon liqueur
1 part Malibu Coconut Rum®
1 part pineapple juice
Shake with ice and strain into a shot glass.

ALL FALL DOWN
1 part tequila blanco
1 part coffee liqueur
1 part dark rum
Shake with ice and strain into a shot glass.

ALMOND COOKIE
1 part amaretto
1 part butterscotch schnapps
Shake with ice and strain into a shot glass.

ALMOND JOY SHOOTER
1 part amaretto
1 part Irish cream
1 part dark crème de cacao
Layer in a shot glass.

ALPINE BREEZE
1 part dark rum
1 part peppermint schnapps
1 part pineapple juice
1 part grenadine
Shake with ice and strain into a shot glass.

ALTERED STATE
1 part pear liqueur
1 part Irish cream
1 part coffee liqueur
Layer in a shot glass.

ALTERNATE
1 part crème de cassis
1 part melon liqueur
1 part pineapple juice
Shake with ice and strain into a shot glass.

AMALFI DRIVE
1 part crème de banana
1 part limoncello
Shake with ice and strain into a shot glass.

AMARETTO CHILL
1 part vodka
1 part amaretto
1 part lemonade
1 part pineapple juice
Shake with ice and strain into a shot glass.

AMARETTO KAMIHUZI
1 part tequila
1 part amaretto
Splash of sweet and sour mix
Shake with ice and strain into a shot glass.
Replace amaretto with cherry, peach, blackberry, raspberry, strawberry, or wild berry
schnapps for different kamihuzis.

AMARETTO KAMIKAZE
1 part vodka
1 part amaretto
Splash of sweet and sour mix
Shake with ice and strain into a shot glass.
Replace amaretto with cherry, peach, blackberry, raspberry, strawberry, or wild berry
schnapps for different kamikazes.

AMARETTO LEMON DROP

1 part vodka
1 part amaretto
Splash of lemon juice

Shake with ice and strain into a shot glass.
Replace amaretto with cherry, peach, blackberry, raspberry, strawberry, or wild berry
schnapps for different lemon drops.

AMARETTO POP

1 part amaretto
Splash of club soda

Add splash of club soda to amaretto in a
shot glass. Place napkin or (clean) hand over
glass. Raise 2 to 3 inches, then rap glass
firmly on bar or table. Quickly drink while
the drink is fizzing.

AMARETTO SLAMMER

1 part amaretto
1 part lemon lime soda

Add splash of lemon lime soda to amaretto
in a shot glass. Place napkin or (clean) hand
over glass. Raise 2 to 3 inches then rap glass
firmly on bar or table. Quickly drink while
the drink is fizzing.

AMARETTO SOUR

1 part amaretto
1 part sour mix

Shake with ice and strain into a shot glass.

AMARETTO SOURBALL
1 part vodka
1 part amaretto
Splash of lemon juice
Splash of orange juice
Shake with ice and strain into a shot glass.

AMARETTO SWEET TART
1 part vodka
1 part amaretto
1 part DeKuyper Wilderberry Schnapps®
1 part cherry juice
Splash of lemon juice
Shake with ice and strain into a shot glass.

AMARETTO SWIZZLE

2 parts amaretto
1 part margarita mix
Splash of lemon lime soda
Shake first two with ice and strain into a
shot glass. Top with a splash of lemon
lime soda.

AMERICAN APPLE PIE

1 part cinnamon schnapps
1 part apple juice
Shake with ice and strain into a shot glass.

AMERICAN DREAM

1 part coffee liqueur
1 part amaretto
1 part Frangelico®
1 part dark crème de cacao
Shake with ice and strain into a shot glass.

AMERICAN FLAG
1 part grenadine
1 part white crème de cacao
1 part blue curaçao
Layer in a shot glass.

AMOCO SHOT
1 part 151-proof rum
1 part vodka
1 drop of coffee liqueur
Pour first two ingredients into a glass
neat (do not chill). Top with drop of
coffee liqueur.

ANABOLIC STEROIDS
2 parts triple sec
2 parts melon liqueur
1 part blue curaçao
Shake with ice and strain into a shot glass.

ANDIES

1 part dark crème de cacao
1 part crème de menthe
Shake with ice and strain into a shot glass.

ANEURYSM

1 part ouzo
1 part 100-proof blackberry schnapps
Shake with ice and strain into a shot glass.

ANGEL BLISS

2 parts bourbon
1 part blue curaçao
Splash of 151-proof rum
Layer the first two ingredients
in a shot glass. Top with 151-proof rum.

ANGEL'S KISS

1 part crème de cacao white
1 part brandy
1 part cream
1 part sloe gin
Layer in a shot glass.

ANGEL'S LIPS

1 part Benedictine®
1 part Irish cream
Layer in a shot glass.

ANGEL'S RUSH SHOOTER

1 part Frangelico®
1 part cream
Shake with ice and strain into a shot glass.

ANGEL'S TIT

1 part white crème de cacao
1 part maraschino liqueur
1 part heavy cream
Maraschino cherry

Layer in a shot glass. Chill for a half-hour before serving and garnish with a cherry.

ANGEL'S WING 1

1 part white crème de cacao
1 part brandy

Shake with ice and strain into a shot glass.

ANGEL'S WING 2

1 part white crème de cacao
1 part brandy
1 part Irish cream

Layer in a shot glass.

ANGRY FIJIAN, THE
1 part crème de banana
1 part coconut rum
Shake with ice and strain into a shot glass.

ANGRY GERMAN, THE
1 part amaretto
1 part blackberry schnapps
1 part Jägermeister®
2 parts lime juice
Dash of salt
Shake with ice and strain into a shot glass.

ANONYMOUS
1 part Southern Comfort®
1 part raspberry liqueur
1 part sweet and sour mix
Shake with ice and strain into a shot glass.

ANTIFREEZE 1
1 part vodka
1 part green crème de menthe
Shake with ice and strain into a shot glass.

ANTIFREEZE 2
2 parts vodka
1 part melon liqueur
Splash of lemon lime soda
Shake with ice and strain into a shot glass.

ANTIFREEZE 3
1 part vodka
1 part blue curaçao
Splash of lemon juice
Splash of margarita mix
Shake with ice and strain into a shot glass.

ANUS BURNER
1 part tequila
1 slice of jalapeño pepper
Dash of hot sauce
Place slice of jalapeño pepper in a shot glass. Add tequila. Add dashes of hot sauce until the shot is a deep red color.

APPLE CHILL
2 parts sour apple schnapps
1 part pineapple juice
Dash of lemon juice
Shake with ice and strain into a shot glass.

APPLE AND CINNAMON JOY
1 part sour apple schnapps
Dash of Goldschläger®
Pour schnapps into shot glass. Dribble
Goldschläger® into schnapps. Stir.

APPLE COBBLER
1 part sour apple schnapps
1 part Goldschläger®
1 part Irish cream
Shake with ice and strain into a shot glass.

APPLE LIMEDROP
1 part vodka
1 part triple sec
Splash of margarita mix
Dash of apple juice
Shake with ice and strain into a shot glass.

APPLE MULE

1 part amaretto
1 part whiskey
1 part Southern Comfort®
1 part triple sec
1 part lime juice
1 part orange juice
Shake with ice and strain into a shot glass.*
*Note: Because this recipe includes many ingredients,
it's easier to make in volume, about 6 shots.

APPLE PIE 1

1 part cinnamon schnapps
1 part sour apple schnapps
Shake with ice and strain into a shot glass.

APPLE PIE 2

1 part apple sauce
1 part vodka
Shake with ice and strain into a shot glass.

APPLE PIE 3

1 part apple juice
1 part vodka
Dash of cinnamon schnapps
Shake with ice and strain into a shot glass.
Garnish with whipped cream.

APPLE PIE 4

1 part Irish Mist®
1 part cinnamon schnapps
1 part Frangelico®
1 part amaretto
Shake with ice and strain into a shot glass.

APPLE RANCHER 1

1 part sour apple schnapps
1 part sweet and sour mix
1 part bourbon
Shake with ice and strain into a shot glass.

APPLE RANCHER 2

1 part sour apple schnapps
1 part triple sec
1 part citrus vodka
Splash of lemon lime soda
Splash of sweet and sour mix
Shake with ice and strain into a shot glass.*

*Note: Because this recipe includes many ingredients,
it's easier to make in volume, about 6 shots.

APPLE SLAMMER

1 part lemon lime soda
1 part sour apple schnapps
Pour ingredients into a glass neat (do not chill). Cover glass tightly with hand, slam on the bar, then drink while it is still fizzing.

APPLE TART
1 part vodka
1 part sour apple schnapps
1 part cherry juice
1 part DeKuyper Wilderberry Schnapps®
Splash of lemon juice
Shake with ice and strain into a shot glass.

APPLECAKE
1 part Licor 43®
1 part apple schnapps
1 part milk
Shake with ice and strain into a shot glass.

APRICOT CHILL
2 parts apricot brandy
1 part lemon juice
1 part pineapple juice
Shake with ice and strain into a shot glass.

APRICOT SOURBALL
1 part vodka
1 part apricot brandy
Splash of lemon juice
Splash of orange juice
Shake with ice and strain into a shot glass.

AQUA FRESH
1 part red cinnamon schnapps
1 part 100-proof peppermint schnapps
1 part blue peppermint schnapps
Layer in a shot glass.

AQUA DEL FUEGO
1 part tequila
1 part hot sauce
Pour ingredients into a glass neat
(do not chill).

ARE YOU TOUGH ENOUGH?

1 part 100-proof cinnamon schnapps
1 part 100-proof vodka
1 part 100-proof peppermint schnapps
1 part 100-proof scotch
1 part 100-proof tequila
Shake with ice and strain into a shot glass.*

*Note: Because this recipe includes many ingredients,
it's easier to make in volume, about 6 shots.

ARIZONA POWWOW

1 part red cinnamon schnapps
1 part tequila
1 part light rum
Dash of club soda
Shake first three with ice and strain into a
shot glass. Top with club soda.

ARIZONA TWISTER

1 part vodka
1 part Malibu Coconut Rum®
1 part tequila
Splash of orange juice
Splash of pineapple juice
Splash of crème de coconut
Dash of grenadine
Shake with ice and strain into a shot glass.*

Note: Because this recipe includes many ingredients,
it's easier to make in volume, about 6 shots.

ARMY GREEN

1 part Goldschläger®
1 part Jägermeister®
1 part tequila
Shake with ice and strain into a shot glass.

ASHLEY, THE

1 part amaretto
1 part Irish cream
1 part coconut rum
Shake with ice and strain into a shot glass.

ASPHALT

1 part beer
1 part blackberry liqueur
1 part chocolate syrup
Shake with ice and strain into a shot glass.

ASS

1 part vodka
1 part green crème de menthe
1 part sambuca
Shake with ice and strain into a shot glass.

ASTRONAUT SHOOTER
1 part vodka (chilled)
1 lemon wedge
Sugar
Powdered instant coffee

Shake vodka with ice and strain into a shot glass. Coat the lemon wedge with sugar on one side and coffee on the other, suck the lemon, and drink the chilled vodka.

ASTROPOP 1
1 part Yukon Jack®
1 part Goldschläger®
1 part melon liqueur
1 part grenadine

Shake with ice and strain into a shot glass.

ASTROPOP 2

1 part grenadine
1 part amaretto
1 part 100-proof peppermint schnapps
Layer in a shot glass.

A.T.B. (ASK THE BARMAN)

1 part melon liqueur
1 part grenadine
1 part blue curaçao
1 part amaretto
1 part Irish cream
Layer in a shot glass.

ATOM BOMB

1 part sour apple schnapps
1 part Goldschläger®
Shake with ice and strain into a shot glass.

ATOMIC BOMB SHOOTER
1 part rye whiskey
1 part tequila
Layer in a shot glass.

ATOMIC SHOT, THE
1 part tequila blanco
1 part Goldschläger®
1 part pepper-flavored vodka
1 part soda water
Shake with ice and strain into a shot glass.

AVALANCHE SHOT
1 part brown crème de cacao
1 part coffee liqueur
1 part Southern Comfort®
Shake with ice and strain into a shot glass.

B2 BOMBER

1 part rum
1 part Southern Comfort®
Splash of lemon lime soda
Splash of lemon lime sports drink
Shake with ice and strain into a shot glass.

B-51

1 part Irish cream
1 part coffee liqueur
1 part rum
Layer in a shot glass.

B-52 1
1 part coffee liqueur
1 part amaretto
1 part Irish cream
Layer in a shot glass.

B-52 2
1 part coffee liqueur
1 part Irish cream
1 part Grand Marnier®
Layer in a shot glass.

B-52 3
1 part coffee liqueur
1 part Irish cream
1 part Cointreau®
Layer in a shot glass.

B-52 4

1 part Irish cream
1 part Tia Maria®
1 part absinthe
Layer in a shot glass.

B-52 5

1 part Irish cream
1 part Tia Maria®
1 part Grand Marnier®
Layer in a shot glass.

B-52 6

1 part Irish cream
2 parts amaretto
1 part dark rum
Layer in a shot glass.

B-52 WITH BOMBAY DOORS

1 part Irish cream
1 part coffee liqueur
1 part Grand Marnier®
1 part Bombay Gin®
Layer in a shot glass.

B-53

1 part coffee liqueur
1 part sambuca
1 part Grand Marnier®
Layer in a shot glass.

B-54

1 part Irish cream
1 part green crème de menthe
1 part Grand Marnier®
1 part coffee liqueur
Shake with ice and strain into a shot glass.

BABY GUINNESS

1 part coffee liqueur
Splash of Irish cream
Pour coffee liqueur in a shot glass.
Float Irish cream on top.
It looks like a miniature draft Guinness®.

BACK DRAFT

1 part tequila
1 part Grand Marnier®
4 dashes of hot sauce
Pour tequila into a shot glass and then
pour in the Grand Marnier®. Then put in
the dashes of hot sauce and let them
settle to the bottom. If you think you're
safe when you taste the tequila and the
Grand Marnier®, just wait for the back
draft of the hot sauce.

BACK SHOT
2 parts vodka
1 part sweet and sour mix
1 part raspberry liqueur
Shake with ice and strain into a shot glass.

BACKFIRE
1 part coffee liqueur
1 part Irish cream
1 part vodka
Layer in a shot glass.

BACKSTREET ROMEO
1 part whiskey
1 part Irish cream
Shake with ice and strain into a shot glass.

BAD STING

1 part grenadine
1 part anisette
1 part Grand Marnier®
1 part tequila
Layer in a shot glass.

BAGHDAD CAFE

1 part coffee liqueur
1 part Tia Maria®
1 part San Marco Cream® liqueur
Layer in a shot glass.

BAILEYS CHOCOLATE-COVERED CHERRY

1 part grenadine
1 part coffee liqueur
1 part Baileys Irish Cream®
Layer in a shot glass.

BAILEY'S COMET

1 part Baileys Irish Cream®
1 part Goldschläger®
Splash of 151-proof rum
Layer the first two ingredients in a shot
glass. Top with 151-proof rum.

BAILEY'S SUNSET

1 part coffee liqueur
1 part Irish cream
1 part triple sec
Layer in a shot glass.

BAISER D'ANGE

1 part white crème de cacao
1 part Parfait Amour®
1 part triple sec
Layer in a shot glass.

BALD EAGLE SHOOTER
1 part 100-proof peppermint schnapps
1 part gold tequila
Shake with ice and strain into a shot glass.

BALD-HEADED WOMAN
3 parts 151-proof rum
1 part grapefruit juice
Shake with ice and strain into a shot glass.

BALL HOOTER
1 part tequila
1 part peppermint schnapps
Shake with ice and strain into a shot glass.

BALLISTIC MISSILE
1 part amaretto
1 part Grand Marnier®
1 part pineapple juice
Shake with ice and strain into a shot glass.

BANANA BOAT SHOOTER
1 part 100-proof peppermint schnapps
1 part coffee liqueur
1 part crème de banana
Shake with ice and strain into a shot glass.

BANANA BOMBER
1 part banana liqueur
1 part triple sec
Splash of grenadine
Shake with ice and strain into a shot glass.

BANANA BOOMER SHOOTER
1 part rum
1 part banana liqueur
1 part lemon juice
1 part orange juice
1 part pineapple juice
Shake with ice and strain into a shot glass.*
Note: Because this recipe includes many ingredients,
it's easier to make in volume, about 6 shots.

BANANA CREAM PIE 1
1 part banana liqueur
1 part white crème de cacao
1 part vodka
1 part half 'n half
Shake with ice and strain into a shot glass.

BANANA CREAM PIE 2
1 part coffee liqueur
1 part Licor 43®
1 part 99-proof banana liqueur
Layer in a shot glass.

BANANA DROP
1 part crème de banana
1 part Irish cream
Splash of light cream
Splash of chocolate mint liqueur
Shake with ice and strain into a shot glass.

BANANA REPUBLIC
2 parts crème de banana
1 part banana juice
1 part sugar syrup
Shake with ice and strain into a shot glass.

BANANA SLUG

3 parts 99-proof banana liqueur
1 part pineapple juice
Shake with ice and strain into a shot glass.

BANANA SOURBALL

1 part vodka
1 part banana schnapps
Splash of lemonade
Splash of orange juice
Shake with ice and strain into a shot glass.

BANANA SPLIT

1 part Swiss chocolate almond liqueur
1 part strawberry liqueur
1 part banana liqueur
Layer in a shot glass.

BANANARAMA
1 part vodka
1 part crème de banana
Shake with ice and strain into a shot glass.

BANANAS AND CREAM
1 part coffee liqueur
1 part Irish cream
1 part 99-proof banana liqueur
Shake with ice and strain into a shot glass.

BANDERA (SPANISH FOR "FLAG")

1 part lime juice
1 part tequila
1 part tomato juice

Take three shot glasses and line them up in front of you, filling one with lime juice, one with tequila, and one with tomato juice, in that order (to represent the Mexican flag). Start at the lime juice and shoot them all quickly in order.

BANDITO

1 part banana liqueur
1 part milk

Shake with ice and strain into a shot glass.

BANSHEE BAMBOO
1 part crème de banana
1 part white crème de cacao
1 part cream
Shake with ice and strain into a shot glass.

BANSHEE BERRY
1 part crème de banana
1 part white crème de cacao
1 part strawberry liqueur
Shake with ice and strain into a shot glass.

BARBADOS BLAST
1 part dark rum
1 part blue curaçao
1 part ginger liqueur
Shake with ice and strain into a shot glass.

BARBED WIRE
1 part Goldschläger®
1 part sambuca
Shake with ice and strain into a shot glass.

BARFING SENSATIONS
1 part blackberry liqueur
1 part peach schnapps
1 part vodka
1 part apple brandy
1 part raspberry liqueur
Shake with ice and strain into a shot glass.*
*Note: Because this recipe includes many ingredients,
it's easier to make in volume, about 6 shots.

BARNEY ON ACID
1 part blue curaçao
1 part Jägermeister®
Splash of cranberry juice cocktail
Shake with ice and strain into a shot glass.

BARTENDER'S WET DREAM
1 part grenadine
1 part coffee liqueur
1 part Irish cream
Shake with ice and strain into a shot glass.
Garnish with whipped cream.

BAT BITE
1 part Bacardi® rum
1 part cranberry juice cocktail
Shake with ice and strain into a shot glass.
This comes from the Bacardi bat logo,
attributed to the bats that lived in the
caves where Bacardi® rum was aged.

BATTERED, BRUISED, AND BLEEDING
1 part grenadine
1 part melon liqueur
1 part blue curaçao
Layer in a shot glass.

BAYOU JUICE
1 part Malibu Coconut Rum®
1 part Captain Morgan's Spiced Rum®
1 part amaretto
1 part cranberry juice cocktail
1 part pineapple juice
Shake with ice and strain into a shot glass.*
*Note: Because this recipe includes many ingredients,
it's easier to make in volume, about 6 shots.

B.B.C.

1 part Benedictine®
1 part Baileys Irish Cream®
1 part Cointreau®
Layer in a shot glass.

B.B.G

1 part Benedictine®
1 part Baileys Irish Cream®
1 part Grand Marnier®
Layer in a shot glass.

BEAM ME UP, SCOTTY

1 part coffee liqueur
1 part Irish cream
1 part banana liqueur
Layer in a shot glass.

BEARCAT SPECIAL
1 part 151-proof rum
1 part peppermint schnapps
Pour ingredients into a glass neat
(do not chill).

BEAUTIFUL
1 part Grand Marnier®
1 part Courvoisier®
Layer in a shot glass.

BEAUTY AND THE BEAST
3 parts Jägermeister®
1 part Tequila Rose®
Layer in a shot glass.

BEAVER BLAST
1 part light rum
1 part dark rum
1 part spiced rum
Shake with ice and strain into a shot glass.

BELFAST BOMBER
1 part Irish whiskey
1 part cognac
1 part vanilla schnapps
Shake with ice and strain into a shot glass.

BELLEVUE GANGBANG
1 part Goldschläger®
1 part black sambuca
Layer in a shot glass.

BEND ME OVER
1 part bourbon
1 part amaretto
1 part sweet and sour mix
Shake with ice and strain into a shot glass.

BERRY BLAST
1 part strawberry juice
1 part vodka
Shake with ice and strain into a shot glass.

BETTY COME BACK
3 parts silver tequila
2 parts triple sec
1 part Parfait Amour®
Shake with ice and strain into a shot glass.

BEVERLY HILLS
1 part Swiss chocolate almond liqueur
1 part Irish cream
1 part Grand Marnier®
Layer in a shot glass.

BIANCA POP, THE
1 part coconut rum
1 part amaretto
Layer in a shot glass.

BIG BALLER
2 parts vodka
1 part gin
1 part triple sec
2 drops of lemon extract
Shake the first three ingredients with ice and
strain into a shot glass. Top with two drops
of lemon extract.

BIG O
1 part peppermint schnapps
1 part Irish cream
Layer in a shot glass.

BIG ROLLER
1 part amaretto
1 part coffee liqueur
1 part crème de banana
Shake with ice and strain into a shot glass.

BIG UNIT
1 part tequila
Splash of blue curaçao
Layer in a shot glass.

BIG V, THE
1 part white crème de cacao
1 part blue curaçao
1 part vodka
1 part sour mix
Layer in a shot glass.

BIKINI LINE
1 part vodka
1 part Tia Maria®
1 part raspberry liqueur
Shake with ice and strain into a shot glass.

BILLY BAD ASS
1 part 151-proof rum
1 part tequila
1 part Jägermeister®
Shake with ice and strain into a shot glass.

BIONIC BEAVER
1 part vodka
1 part Southern Comfort®
1 part sloe gin
1 part gin
1 part grenadine
Shake with ice and strain into a shot glass.

BIPPLE
1 part butterscotch schnapps
1 part Irish cream
Layer in a shot glass.

BIRD SHIT
1 part blackberry brandy
Splash of tequila
Dash of milk

Fill shot glass about three-fourths full of
blackberry brandy. Float the tequila on top
of the brandy. Pour in a little bit of milk
for effect. Look familiar?

BIT 'O HONEY
1 part butterscotch schnapps
1 part Irish cream
Shake with ice and strain into a shot glass.

BITCHIN'
1 part triple sec
1 part peach schnapps
1 part melon liqueur
Shake with ice and strain into a shot glass.

BITE OF THE IGUANA

1 part tequila
1 part triple sec
1 part vodka
Splash of orange juice
Splash of sour mix
Shake with ice and strain into a shot glass.

BLACK ARMY

1 part Galliano®
1 part Jägermeister®
Layer in a shot glass.

BLACK AND BLUE

1 part tequila
1 part blue curaçao
1 part raspberry schnapps
Shake with ice and strain into a shot glass.

BLACK DEATH
1 part Jack Daniel's®
1 part tequila
Shake with ice and strain into a shot glass.

BLACK DEVIL
1 part dark rum
1 part crème de menthe
Layer in a shot glass.

BLACK DRAGON
1 part crème de menthe
1 part coffee liqueur
1 part scotch
Layer in a shot glass.

BLACK FOREST CAKE

1 part cherry brandy
1 part coffee liqueur
1 part Irish cream
Shake with ice and strain into a shot glass.

BLACK GOLD SHOOTER

1 part black sambuca
1 part Goldschläger®
Shake with ice and strain into a shot glass.

BLACK HOLE

1 part Jägermeister®
1 part 100-proof peppermint schnapps
Make certain that the Jägermeister® is as
cold as possible. Pour the Jäger into a shot
glass and top with peppermint schnapps.
The peppermint schnapps will sink to the
bottom giving a "black hole" effect.

BLACK JACK
1 part coffee liqueur
1 part anisette
Layer in a shot glass.

BLACK JACK WV
3 parts Yukon Jack®
1 part raspberry liqueur
1 part sour mix
Splash of lemon lime soda
Shake with ice and strain into a shot glass.

BLACK KENTUCKY
1 part whiskey
1 part black sambuca
Layer in a shot glass.

BLACK ORGASM

1 part sloe gin
1 part blue curaçao
1 part peach schnapps
1 part vodka
Shake with ice and strain into a shot glass.

BLACK PEPPER

1 part pepper-flavored vodka
1 part blackberry liqueur
Shake with ice and strain into a shot glass.

BLACK RAIN

1 part black sambuca
3 parts champagne
Pour ingredients into a glass.

BLACK SAMURAI
2 parts sake
1 part soy sauce
Pour ingredients into a glass neat
(do not chill).

BLACK SAND
1 part coffee liqueur
1 part sambuca
1 part amaretto
Layer in a shot glass.

BLACK TIE
1 part Drambuie®
1 part scotch
1 part amaretto
Layer in a shot glass.

BLACK ON WHITE
1 part black sambuca
1 part white sambuca
Layer in a shot glass.

BLACK WIDOW
1 part black sambuca
1 part strawberry schnapps
1 part cream
Layer in a shot glass.

BLACK WOLF
1 part black sambuca
1 part Green Chartreuse®
4 drops of hot sauce
Layer in a shot glass.

BLASTER
1 part banana liqueur
1 part triple sec
1 part coffee liqueur
Layer in a shot glass.

BLEACHER CREATURE
1 part butterscotch schnapps
1 part 151-proof rum
Layer in a shot glass.

BLEACHER'S TWIST
1 part coffee liqueur
1 part raspberry liqueur
1 part Irish cream
Layer in a shot glass.

BLEEDIN' HELL
3 parts vodka
2 parts strawberry schnapps
1 part lemonade
Shake with ice and strain into a shot glass.

BLISTER IN THE SUN
1 part Windsor Canadian Whisky®
1 part raspberry liqueur
1 part orange juice
1 part lemon juice
1 part lemon lime soda
Shake with ice and strain into a shot glass.*
*Note: Because this recipe includes many ingredients,
it's easier to make in volume, about 6 shots.

BLOOD CLOT 1
1 part Southern Comfort®
Splash of grenadine
Pour ingredients into a glass neat
(do not chill).

BLOOD CLOT 2
1 part light rum
1 part cream
Splash of grenadine
Layer in a shot glass. Grenadine will sink
to the bottom.

BLOODY BRAIN
1 part peach schnapps
Splash of Irish cream
2 to 3 drops of grenadine
Pour the first two ingredients into a shot
glass and add drops of grenadine.

BLOODY FROG CUM
1 part grenadine
1 part light rum
1 part melon liqueur
Splash of Irish cream
Layer the grenadine, rum, and melon in a
shot glass. Slowly dribble the Irish cream
into the bottom of the glass, letting it collect.

BLOODY STOOL
1 part Campari®
1 part Irish cream
1 part lime juice
1 part 151-proof rum
Pour ingredients into a glass neat
(do not chill).

BLOODY SUNDAY
1 part tropical schnapps
1 part grenadine
1 part piña colada mix
1 part vodka
Shake with ice and strain into a shot glass.

BLOW JOB (SKILLED)
1 part vodka
1 part coffee liqueur
1 part Irish cream
1 part crème de banana
Layer in a shot glass. Garnish with whipped
cream. Drink without using your hands!

BLOW JOB 1

1 part coffee liqueur
1 part amaretto
Layer in a shot glass. Garnish with whipped cream. Drink without using your hands!

BLOW JOB 2

1 part Irish cream
1 part crème de banana
Layer in a shot glass. Garnish with whipped cream. Drink without using your hands!

BLOW JOB 3

1 part coffee liqueur
1 part Irish cream
Layer in a shot glass. Garnish with whipped cream. Drink without using your hands!

BLOW JOB 4
1 part Irish cream
1 part Grand Marnier®
1 part crème de banana
Layer in a shot glass. Garnish with whipped cream. Drink without using your hands!

BLOW JOB 5
1 part coffee liqueur
1 part vodka
Layer in a shot glass. Garnish with whipped cream. Drink without using your hands!

BLUE BALLS 1
1 part blue curaçao
1 part Malibu Coconut Rum®
1 part peach schnapps
1 splash sweet and sour mix
Dash of lemon lime soda
Shake with ice and strain into a shot glass.

BLUE BALLS 2
1 part gin
1 part blue curaçao
1 part melon liqueur
Shake with ice and strain into a shot glass.

BLUE BANANA
1 part crème de banana
1 part blue curaçao
Layer in a shot glass.

BLUE CABOOSE
1 part Irish cream
1 part whiskey
1 part amaretto
Layer in a shot glass.

BLUE ICE
1 part blue curaçao
1 part citrus vodka
Layer in a shot glass.

BLUE KISOK
2 parts blue curaçao
1 part vodka
Splash of lime juice
Splash of lemon lime soda
Shake the first three ingredients with ice
and strain into a shot glass. Top with
lemon lime soda.

BLUE LEMON DROP
1 part vodka
1 part blue curaçao
Splash of lemonade
Shake with ice and strain into a shot glass.

BLUE MARBLE
1 part black sambuca
1 part light rum
1 part cream
1 part gin
Layer in a shot glass.

BLUE MARLIN
2 parts light rum
1 part blue curaçao
1 part lime juice
Shake with ice and strain into a shot glass.

BLUE MEANIE

1 part blue curaçao
1 part vodka
1 part sweet and sour mix
Shake with ice and strain into a shot glass.

BLUE MOON

1 part amaretto
1 part Irish cream
1 part blue curaçao
Layer in a shot glass.

BLUE NEON

3 parts Goldschläger®
1 part 151-proof rum
1 splash blue curaçao
Layer in a shot glass.

BLUE NUT
1 part blueberry schnapps
1 part Frangelico®
Shake with ice and strain into a shot glass.

BLUE PEACH
2 parts peach schnapps
1 part blue curaçao
Shake with ice and strain into a shot glass.

BLUE POLAR BEAR
1 part vodka
1 part Avalanche® peppermint schnapps
Shake with ice and strain into a shot glass.

BLUE SIG
2 parts blue curaçao
1 part triple sec
1 part vodka
Shake with ice and strain into a shot glass.

BLUE SMURF PISS
1 part Jägermeister®
1 part 151-proof rum
1 part 100-proof peppermint schnapps
1 part Goldschläger®
1 part blue curaçao
Shake with ice and strain into a shot glass.*
*Note: Because this recipe includes many ingredients,
it's easier to make in volume, about 6 shots.

BLUE SOURBALL
1 part vodka
2 parts blue curaçao
Splash of lemonade
Splash of orange juice
Shake with ice and strain into a shot glass.

BLUE THRILL
1 part blue curaçao
1 part lemon juice
Layer in a shot glass.

BLUEBERRY WATERFALL
1 part blueberry schnapps
1 part orange juice
Layer in a shot glass.

BLUE-EYED BLONDE

1 part banana liqueur
1 part blue curaçao
1 part Irish cream
Layer in a shot glass.

BLURRICANE

1 part blue curaçao
1 part 100-proof peppermint schnapps
1 part Goldschläger®
1 part Jägermeister®
1 part Wild Turkey®
1 part ouzo
Shake with ice and strain into a shot glass.*

*Note: Because this recipe includes many ingredients,
it's easier to make in volume, about 6 shots.

BOB MARLEY

1 part melon liqueur
1 part Jägermeister®
1 part Goldschläger®
Layer in a shot glass.

BODY SHOT

1 part vodka
1 sugar packet
1 lemon wedge

Using a partner, lick his or her neck to moisten. Pour the packet of sugar onto his or her neck. Place wedge of lemon in his or her mouth, with the skin pointed inward. You first lick the sugar from the neck, then shoot the vodka, then suck the lemon from his or her mouth (while gently holding back of the neck).

BOILER MAKER
1 12-ounce beer
1 shot glass of whiskey
Fill a glass with 12 ounces of beer. Hold the
shot glass of whiskey above the beer glass,
drop it in, and chug.
P.S.: Don't break a tooth on the shot glass!

BOMB, THE
1 part sour apple schnapps
1 part peach schnapps
1 part banana liqueur
1 part pineapple juice
1 part lemon lime soda
Shake with ice and strain into a shot glass.*
*Note: Because this recipe contains many ingredients,
it's easier to make in volume, about 6 shots.

BONFIRE
3 parts Irish cream
1 part Goldschläger®
Dash of cinnamon
Layer in a shot glass.

BONG WATER 1
1 part melon liqueur
1 part orange juice
1 part Jägermeister®
Shake with ice and strain into a shot glass.

BONG WATER 2
1 part vodka
1 part orange juice
1 part sweet and sour mix
1 part grape juice
Shake with ice and strain into a shot glass.

BONGS ANFIELD SLAMMER
1 part vodka
1 part Irish cream
1 part coffee
1 part milk
Shake with ice and strain into a shot glass.

BONONO
1 part banana liqueur
1 part triple sec
1 part Grand Marnier®
Layer in a shot glass.

BONSAI PIPELINE 1
3 parts Wild Turkey 101®
3 parts melon liqueur
1 part 151-proof rum
Layer in a shot glass.

BONSAI PIPELINE 2
1 part vodka
1 part tropical schnapps
Shake with ice and strain into a shot glass.

BOOGER
1 part Malibu Coconut Rum®
1 part banana liqueur
1 part melon liqueur
Splash of Irish cream
Shake the first three ingredients with ice
and strain into a shot glass. Top with splash
of Irish cream.

BOOGERS IN THE GRASS
1 part melon liqueur
1 part peach schnapps
Dash of Irish cream
Shake the first three ingredients with ice
and strain into a shot glass. Top with dash
of Irish cream in the center of the shot.

BOOK ME AN AMBULANCE
1 part Yellow Chartreuse®
1 part cherry brandy
1 part absinthe
Layer in a shot glass.

BOOM-BOX
1 part Smirnoff® vodka
1 part white wine
1 part hot coffee
Layer in a shot glass.

BOOMER
1 part tequila
1 part triple sec
1 part crème de banana
1 part orange juice
1 part sour mix
Shake with ice and strain into a shot glass.*
*Note: Because this recipe includes many ingredients,
it's easier to make in volume, about 6 shots.

BOOMERANG SHOT
1 part Jägermeister®
1 part Yukon Jack®
Layer in a shot glass.

BOOTLEGGER, THE
1 part whiskey
1 part Southern Comfort®
1 part sambuca
Shake with ice and strain into a shot glass.

BOSWANDELING (A WALK IN THE WOODS)
1 part vodka
1 part triple sec
5 dashes of Angostura® bitters
Shake with ice and strain into a shot glass.

BOTTOM BOUNCER
1 part Irish cream
1 part butterscotch schnapps
Layer in a shot glass.

B.P. RISER
1 part crème de banana
1 part melon liqueur
1 part vodka
Shake with ice and strain into a shot glass.

BRAIN
1 part peach schnapps
1 part Irish cream
Shake with ice and strain into a shot glass.

BRAIN DAMAGE
1 part 151-proof rum
1 part amaretto
Dash of Irish cream
Shake the first two ingredients with ice
and strain into a shot glass.
Top with Irish cream.

BRAIN DEAD
1 part vodka
1 part sour mix
1 part triple sec
Shake with ice and strain into a shot glass.

BRAIN DESTROYER
1 part Irish cream
1 part coffee liqueur
1 part amaretto
Dash of 151-proof rum
Shake the first three ingredients with ice
and strain into a shot glass. Top with
151-proof rum.

BRAIN ERASER
1 part amaretto
1 part coffee liqueur
1 part vodka
Dash of club soda
Fill a glass with ice and add vodka, amaretto, and coffee liqueur. Top off with club
soda. This should be drunk all at once
through a straw.

BRAIN HEMORRHAGE
1 part peach schnapps
Splash of Irish cream
Dash of grenadine
Pour a shot glass three-fourths full with peach schnapps and pour Irish cream into the center of the schnapps, allowing it to clump. Drop the grenadine over the back of a bar spoon into the Irish cream.

BRAINMASTER
1 part light rum
1 part crème de coconut
1 part white crème de cacao
Dash of apricot syrup
Shake with ice and strain into a shot glass.

BRANDED NIPPLE
1 part butterscotch schnapps
1 part Irish cream
1 part Goldschläger®
Dash of 151-proof rum
Layer in a shot glass.

BRASS BALLS
1 part Grand Marnier®
1 part peach schnapps
1 part pineapple juice
Shake with ice and strain into a shot glass.

BRAVE BULL 1
1 part tequila
1 part hot sauce
Layer in a shot glass.

BRAVE BULL 2
1 part tequila
1 part coffee liqueur
Layer in a shot glass.

BREATH FRESHENER
1 part vodka
2 parts peppermint schnapps
1 peppermint candy
Place the peppermint candy in the bottom of
the glass. Add the vodka first and then fill
with the peppermint liqueur.

BREATHALYZER
1 part peppermint schnapps
1 part light rum
Shake with ice and strain into a shot glass.

BROKEN DOWN GOLF CART

1 part amaretto
1 part melon liqueur
1 part cranberry juice cocktail
Shake with ice and strain into a shot glass.

BRUISED HEART

1 part vodka
1 part raspberry liqueur
1 part peach schnapps
1 part cranberry juice cocktail
Shake with ice and strain into a shot glass.

BS

1 part coffee liqueur
1 part Irish cream
1 part Grand Marnier®
Shake with ice and strain into a shot glass.

BUBBLE

1 part amaretto
1 part crème de banana
1 part melon liqueur
1 part cream
Shake with ice and strain into a shot glass.

BUBBLE GUM

1 part Southern Comfort®
1 part amaretto
1 part banana liqueur
1 part milk
1 part grenadine
Shake with ice and strain into a shot glass.

BUCKSHOT
1 part tequila
1 part whiskey
1 part Irish cream
Pinch of fresh ground pepper
Shake whiskey and tequila with ice and strain into a shot glass. Top with Irish cream and garnish with black pepper.

BUDDINS
1 part butterscotch schnapps
1 part Galliano®
1 part Irish cream
Layer in a shot glass.

BUFFALO SWEAT
1 part Yukon Jack®
Splash of hot sauce
Layer in a shot glass.

BULL SHOOT

1 part coffee liqueur
1 part light rum
1 part tequila
Layer in a shot glass.

BUMBLEBEE

1 part Irish cream
1 part coffee liqueur
1 part sambuca
Layer in a shot glass.

BUONASERA SHOOTER

1 part amaretto
1 part coffee liqueur
1 part vanilla rum
Shake with ice and strain into a shot glass.

BURNING CHERRY

1 part bourbon
1 part whiskey
1 part scotch
Dash of grenadine
Pour ingredients into a glass neat (do not chill). Top with grenadine.

BURNING WORM

1 part mescal
1 part Goldschläger®
Layer in a shot glass.

BUSTED CHERRY

1 part coffee liqueur
1 part cherry brandy
Shake with ice and strain into a shot glass.

BUTTER BABY
1 part butterscotch schnapps
1 part Irish cream
Layer in a shot glass.

BUTTERY NIPPLE
1 part butterscotch schnapps
1 part Irish cream
Layer in a shot glass.

BUTTERY NIPPLE WITH AN ATTITUDE
1 part Irish cream
1 part butterscotch schnapps
Dash of peppermint schnapps
Layer in a shot glass.

BUTTERY NIPPLE WITH A CHERRY KISS
1 part butterscotch schnapps
1 part Irish cream
Splash of cherry liqueur
Layer in a shot glass.

BUTTMEISTER
3 parts Jägermeister®
1 part butterscotch schnapps
Shake with ice and strain into a shot glass.

BUZZARD'S BREATH
1 part peppermint schnapps
1 part amaretto
1 part coffee liqueur
Shake with ice and strain into a shot glass.

CACTUS THORN
2 parts silver tequila
1 part green crème de menthe
1 part lime juice (freshly squeezed)
Shake with ice and strain into a shot glass.

CALIFORNIA SURFER
1 part Jägermeister®
2 parts pineapple juice
1 part Malibu Coconut Rum®
Shake with ice and strain into a shot glass.

CALYPSO COOLER
1 part spiced rum
1 part amaretto
1 part orange juice
Dash of grenadine
Shake with ice and strain into a shot glass.
Top with grenadine.

CAM SHAFT
1 part Irish cream
1 part Jägermeister®
1 part root beer schnapps
Shake with ice and strain into a shot glass.

CANDY CANE
1 part grenadine
1 part crème de menthe
1 part peppermint schnapps
Layer in a shot glass.

CANDY KILLER WITH A KISS

1 part ouzo
1 part Jägermeister®
1 part Goldschläger®
Layer in a shot glass.

CAPTAIN LOUIE

1 part spiced rum
1 drop of vanilla extract
1 part coffee liqueur
1 drop of vanilla extract
Layer in a shot glass.

CARAMILK

2 parts white crème de cacao
1 part crème de banana
1 part coffee liqueur
Layer in a shot glass.

CARROT CAKE
1 part butterscotch schnapps
1 part Irish cream
1 part Goldschläger®
Shake with ice and strain into a shot glass.

CATFISH
3 parts bourbon
1 part peach schnapps
Shake with ice and strain into a shot glass.

CELL, THE
1 part apricot brandy
1 part cachaca
1 part vanilla schnapps
Shake with ice and strain into a shot glass.

CELT, THE

2 parts blueberry schnapps
1 part scotch
Shake with ice and strain into a shot glass.

CEMENT MIXER

1 part Irish cream
1 part sweetened lime juice
Layer the lime juice on top of the Irish cream. The lime juice will cause the Irish cream to curdle. Take the shot and swish it around in your mouth before swallowing.

C'EST L'AMOUR

2 parts rum

1 part blue curaçao

1 part cream

1 part advocaat

Splash of grenadine

Shake with ice and strain into a shot glass.*

Note: Because this recipe includes many ingredients,
it's easier to make in volume, about 6 shots.

CHAMPERELLE

1 part triple sec

1 part anisette

1 part cognac

Shake with ice and strain into a shot glass.

CHASTITY BELT

2 parts Tia Maria®
1 part Frangelico®
1 part Irish cream
Splash of cream
Layer in a shot glass.

CHEESE SARNIE

1 part champagne
1 part crème de cassis
1 part orange vodka
Layer in a shot glass.

CHERRY BLOW

1 part Southern Comfort®
1 part amaretto
1 part grenadine
Shake with ice and strain into a shot glass.

CHERRY BOMB 1
1 part vodka
1 part white crème de cacao
Splash of grenadine
Shake with ice and strain into a shot glass.

CHERRY BOMB 2
1 cherry
2 parts vodka
1 part Goldschläger®
1 part light rum
Shake with ice and strain into a shot glass.

CHERRY CHEESECAKE
1 part vanilla schnapps
1 part cranberry juice cocktail
Shake with ice and strain into a shot glass.

CHERRY SHAKE
1 part Irish cream
1 part cherry liqueur
1 part amaretto
Shake with ice and strain into a shot glass.

CHICKEN DROP
1 part Jägermeister®
1 part peach schnapps
1 part orange juice
Shake with ice and strain into a shot glass.

CHINA WHITE
3 parts white crème de cacao
1 part Irish cream
Pinch of cinnamon powder
Layer in a shot glass. Sprinkle cinnamon
powder on top.

CHIP SHOT
1 part light rum
1 part cranberry juice cocktail
1 part pineapple juice
Shake with ice and strain into a shot glass.

CHOAD
1 part Green Chartreuse®
1 part tequila
Shake with ice and strain into a shot glass.

CHOCOLATE ALMOND
1 part amaretto
1 part dark crème de cacao
1 part Irish cream
Layer in a shot glass.

CHOCOLATE BANANA SHOT
1 part white crème de cacao
1 part crème de banana
Shake with ice and strain into a shot glass.

CHOCOLATE BUZZ
1 part coffee liqueur
1 part Irish cream
1 part chocolate milk
Shake with ice and strain into a shot glass.

CHOCOLATE CHIMP
1 part white crème de cacao
1 part coffee liqueur
1 part crème de banana
Layer in a shot glass.

CHOCOLATE CHIP (SHOOTER)
1 part amaretto
1 part white crème de cacao
1 part Irish cream
Layer in a shot glass.

CHOCOLATE CREAM PEACHES
1 part coffee liqueur
1 part peach schnapps
Shake with ice and strain into a shot glass.

CHOCOLATE GRASSHOPPER
1 part white crème de cacao
1 part crème de menthe
2 parts chocolate milk
Shake with ice and strain into a shot glass.

CHOCOLATE JIZZ

1 part white crème de cacao
1 part coffee liqueur
Shake with ice and strain into a shot glass.

CHOCOLATE MILK

1 part chocolate liqueur
1 part milk
Splash of amaretto
Layer in a shot glass.

CHOCOLATE SUNDAE

1 part Irish cream
1 part white crème de cacao
1 part coffee liqueur
Layer in a shot glass. Top with whipped cream.

CHOCOLATE VALENTINE
1 part vanilla-flavored vodka
1 part dark crème de cacao
1 part cherry juice
Splash of cream
Splash of club soda
Shake with ice and strain into a shot glass.

CHOCOLATE-COVERED CHERRY
1 part coffee liqueur
1 part amaretto
1 part white crème de cacao
1 part cherry juice
Shake with ice and strain into a shot glass.

CHOCOLATE-COVERED RASPBERRY
1 part white crème de cacao
1 part raspberry liqueur
Layer in a shot glass.

CHPOK
2 parts champagne
1 part vodka
Chill vodka separately by shaking it with
ice. Combine ingredients in a shot glass.

CHRISTMAS CHEER
1 part peppermint schnapps
1 part egg nog
Shake with ice and strain into a shot glass.

CHRISTMAS SHOT
1 part melon liqueur
1 part raspberry liqueur
Layer in a shot glass.

CHRISTMAS TREE 1
1 part green crème de menthe
1 part grenadine
1 part Irish cream
Layer in a shot glass.

CHRISTMAS TREE 2
1 part green crème de menthe
1 part vodka
1 part cherry brandy
Layer in a shot glass.

CHUNKY SNAKEBITE
1 part tequila
1 part salsa
Pour ingredients into a glass neat
(do not chill).

CINNAMON APPLE PIE
3 parts sour apple schnapps
1 part cinnamon schnapps
Shake with ice and strain into a shot glass.

CINNAMON STICK
1 part Goldschläger®
1 part apple juice
Shake with ice and strain into a shot glass.

CINNAMON TOAST
1 part Irish cream
1 part Goldschläger®
Shake with ice and strain into a shot glass.

CINNAMON TOAST CRUNCH

1 part butterscotch schnapps
1 part Irish cream
Splash of Goldschläger®
Layer in a shot glass.

CIQUITA

1 part vodka
1 part crème de banana
1 part milk
Shake with ice and strain into a shot glass.

CIRCLE JERK
1 part Irish cream
1 part orange juice
Dash of grenadine
Layer Irish cream and orange juice in a shot glass, allowing the Irish cream to curdle. Carefully pour grenadine along the inside rim of glass, making a circle.

CITRON MY FACE
1 part citrus vodka
1 part triple sec
1 part sour mix
Splash of lemon lime soda
Shake all ingredients, but the soda, with ice and strain into a shot glass. Top with lemon lime soda.

CITRON SOUR
1 part lime juice
1 part citrus vodka
Shake with ice and strain into a shot glass.

CITY HOT SHOT
1 part blue curaçao
1 part triple sec
1 part grenadine
Layer in a shot glass.

CLEAR LAYERED SHOT
1 part lemon lime soda
1 part grain alcohol
1 part grenadine
Combine grain alcohol and lemon lime soda
in a shot glass. Pour grenadine down the
side of the glass. The grenadine should settle
to a layer in the middle of the glass.

CLOSED CASKET
1 part Jägermeister®
1 part 151-proof rum
1 part Firewater®
1 part 100-proof peppermint schnapps
Shake with ice and strain into a shot glass.

COBRA
1 part Irish cream
1 part Jägermeister®
1 part 100-proof peppermint schnapps
Layer in a shot glass.

COBRA'S BITE
1 part pepper-flavored vodka
1 part green crème de menthe
Shake with ice and strain into a shot glass.

COCAINE
1 part vodka
1 part raspberry liqueur
1 part grapefruit juice
Shake with ice and strain into a shot glass.

COCAINE LADY
1 part coffee liqueur
1 part vodka
1 part peppermint schnapps
1 part Irish cream
1 part milk
Shake with ice and strain into a shot glass.

COCKROACH
1 part coffee liqueur
1 part Drambuie®
Shake with ice and strain into a shot glass.

COCMOS

2 parts vodka
1 part fresh lime juice
Shake with ice and strain into a shot glass.

COCONUT CHILL

2 parts coconut rum
1 part lemonade
Splash of pineapple juice
Shake with ice and strain into a shot glass.

COCONUT CREAM PIE

1 part coconut rum
Shake with ice and strain into a shot glass.
Top with whipped cream.

COCONUT LEMON DROP
1 part vodka
1 part coconut rum
Splash of lemonade
Shake with ice and strain into a shot glass.

COCONUT SWEET TART
1 part vodka
1 part coconut rum
1 part cherry juice
Splash of lemonade
Shake with ice and strain into a shot glass.

COCONUT SWIZZLE
2 parts coconut rum
1 part margarita mix
Splash of lemon lime soda
Shake with ice and strain into a shot glass.

COLD VIRGIN

2 parts Southern Comfort®
1 part fresh lime juice
1 part apricot juice
Shake with ice and strain into a shot glass.

COLOMBIAN, THE

1 part coffee liqueur
1 part amaretto
1 part Hennessy®
Shake with ice and strain into a shot glass.

COMA 1

1 part triple sec
1 part coffee liqueur
1 part sambuca
Layer in a shot glass.

COMA 2
1 part dark rum
1 part cinnamon schnapps
Shake with ice and strain into a shot glass.

COMFORT SPECIAL
2 parts Southern Comfort®
1 part sweet vermouth
1 part orange juice
Shake with ice and strain into a shot glass.

COMFORTABLE PUNCH
1 part Southern Comfort®
1 part grenadine
Splash of lemonade
Shake with ice and strain into a shot glass.

CONCORD
1 part coffee liqueur
1 part Irish cream
Splash of 151-proof rum
Layer in a shot glass.

CONTEMPLATOR
1 part citrus vodka
1 teaspoon powdered Tang®
Shake with ice and strain into shot glass.

COOKIE MONSTER
1 part coffee liqueur
1 part Irish cream
1 teaspoon 151-proof rum
Layer in a shot glass.

COOL HOT DAMN

1 part DeKuyper Hot Damn!® cinnamon
schnapps
1 part peppermint schnapps
Shake with ice and strain into a shot glass.

COOTER CORK

2 parts grenadine
2 parts raspberry liqueur
1 part cinnamon schnapps
1 part Absolut Kurant®
Layer in a shot glass.

COPENHAGEN POUSSE-CAFÉ

1 part crème de banana
1 part Cherry Heering®
1 part cognac
Layer in a shot glass.

COPPER CAMEL
1 part Irish cream
1 part butterscotch schnapps
Shake with ice and strain into a shot glass.

CORDLESS SCREWDRIVER
1 part vodka
1 orange wedge
1 teaspoon sugar
Shake vodka with ice and strain into a shot glass. Dip orange wedge in sugar. Shoot the vodka and immediately suck on the orange.

CORRIDOR OF FIRE
2 parts coffee liqueur
1 part cognac
2 parts Irish cream
Layer in a shot glass.

CORTISONE
1 part coffee liqueur
1 part dark rum
Dash of vanilla extract
Shake with ice and strain into a shot glass.

COUGH DROP
1 part peppermint schnapps
1 part blackberry schnapps
Shake with ice and strain into a shot glass.

COUGH SYRUP
1 part blue curaçao
1 part crème de menthe
1 part vodka
Shake with ice and strain into a shot glass.

COWBOY COCKSUCKER
1 part butterscotch schnapps
1 part Irish cream
1 part Southern Comfort®
Shake with ice and strain into a shot glass.

CRASH TEST DUMMY
1 part tequila
1 part triple sec
1 part margarita mix
Shake with ice and strain into a shot glass.

CRAZY GERMAN
1 part Jägermeister®
1 part Rumplemintz®
Shake with ice and strain into a shot glass.

CREAM OF BEEF

1 part Beefeater Gin®
1 part Irish cream
Shake with ice and strain into a shot glass.

CREAM HASH

1 part white crème de cacao
1 part dark rum
Shake with ice and strain into a shot glass.
Top with whipped cream.

CREAM SODA SLAMMER

1 part spiced rum
1 part lemon lime soda
Shake with ice and strain into a shot glass.

CREAMY JONNY

1 part grenadine
1 part Irish cream
1 part milk
1 part raspberry liqueur
Shake with ice and strain into a shot glass.

CREAMY NUTS

1 part crème de banana
1 part Frangelico®
Shake with ice and strain into a shot glass.

CRIMSON TIDE

1 part vodka
1 part coconut rum
1 part raspberry liqueur
1 part tropical schnapps
1 part Southern Comfort®
1 part 151-proof rum
1 part cranberry juice cocktail
1 part lemon lime soda

Shake with ice and strain into a shot glass.*

*Note: Because this recipe includes many ingredients,
it's easier to make in volume, about 6 shots.

CRIPPLER

1 part grain alcohol
1 part 151-proof rum
Splash of triple sec

Shake with ice and strain into a shot glass.

CRISPY CRUNCH

1 part Frangelico®
1 part white crème de cacao
Shake with ice and strain into a shot glass.

CROCKET

2 parts cherry schnapps
1 part sweet and sour mix
Splash of grenadine
Shake with ice and strain into a shot glass.

CROSS-CULTURAL BLACK RUSSIAN

1 part Kahlua®
1 part Tia Maria®
1 part vodka
Layer in a shot glass.

CRUZ AZUL (BLUE CROSS)
1 part 151-proof rum
1 part lemon lime–flavored rum
1 part citrus vodka
1 part 100-proof peppermint schnapps
1 part blue curaçao
Shake with ice and strain into a shot glass.*

Note: Because this recipe includes many ingredients,
it's easier to make in volume, about 6 shots.

CRYSTAL VIRGIN
1 part Yukon Jack®
1 part amaretto
1 part cranberry juice cocktail
Shake with ice and strain into a shot glass.

CUCARACHA 1

1 part vodka
1 part coffee liqueur
1 part tequila
Shake with ice and strain into a shot glass.

CUCARACHA 2

1 part tequila blanco
1 part mineral water
Shake with ice and strain into a shot glass.

CUERVO AZTEC RUIN

1 part Jose Cuervo® tequila
1 part Rose's® sweetened lime juice
Shake with ice and strain into a shot glass.

CUERVO AZTEC SKY
1 part Jose Cuervo® tequila
1 part blue curaçao
Shake with ice and strain into a shot glass.

CUM IN A POND
1 part blue curaçao
1 part vodka
Dash of Irish cream
Shake vodka and blue curaçao with ice and strain into a shot glass. Add a dash of Irish cream to the center.

CUM SCORCHER
1 part butterscotch schnapps
1 part vodka
1 part coffee liqueur
Dash of Irish cream
Layer in a shot glass.

CUM SHOT
1 part butterscotch schnapps
1 part Irish cream
Shake with ice and strain into a shot glass.

CUNNILINGUS
1 part Irish cream
1 part peach schnapps
1 part pineapple juice
Shake with ice and strain into a shot glass.
Top with whipped cream.

CURRANT COOLER SHOT
2 parts currant-flavored vodka
1 part sweet and sour mix
1 part lemon lime soda
Shake with ice and strain into a shot glass.

CURRANT STINGER
1 part Bärenjäger®
1 part currant-flavored vodka
Layer in a shot glass.

CURTAIN CALL
1 part Jägermeister®
1 part melon liqueur
1 part whiskey
Shake with ice and strain into a shot glass.

CYRANO
1 part Irish cream
1 part triple sec
Dash of raspberry liqueur
Layer in a shot glass.

CZECH COLLABORATOR

1 part Goldschläger®
1 part Becherovka®
Shake with ice and strain into a shot glass.
(Becherovka® is an herb-based liqueur made
in the Czech Republic.)

D. O. A. 1
1 part white crème de cacao
1 part peach schnapps
1 part Frangelico®
Shake with ice and strain into a shot glass.

D. O. A. 2
1 part Bärenjäger®
1 part 100-proof peppermint schnapps
1 part Jägermeister®
Layer in a shot glass.

DAGGER

1 part tequila
1 part white crème de cacao
1 part peach schnapps
Layer in a shot glass.

DAKOTA

1 part bourbon
1 part tequila
Pour ingredients into a glass neat
(do not chill).

DALLAS STARS

1 part crème de menthe
1 part Goldschläger®
Layer in a shot glass.

DAMNED IF YOU DO

1 part whiskey
1 part DeKuyper Hot Damn!® cinnamon
schnapps
Pour ingredients into a glass neat
(do not chill).

DANCIN' COWBOY

1 part banana liqueur
1 part coffee liqueur
1 part Irish cream
Layer in a shot glass.

DANGEROUS GRANDMA

2 parts coffee liqueur
1 part whiskey
1 part amaretto
Shake with ice and strain into a shot glass.

DANGEROUS SHOT
1 part crème de banana
1 part light rum
1 part coffee liqueur
1 part dark rum
Shake with ice and strain into a shot glass.

DARK ANGEL
1 part maraschino liqueur
1 part blackberry liqueur
1 part advocaat
Layer in a shot glass.

DARK NIGHTMARE
2 parts coffee liqueur
1 part Goldschläger®
Splash of milk
Shake coffee liqueur and Goldschläger®
with ice and strain into a shot glass. Top
with a splash of milk.

DAVE'S OLIVE BRINE
1 part vodka
1 part olive brine (the liquid in a jar of olives)
1 part grenadine
1 part lemon juice
Pour ingredients into a glass neat
(do not chill).

DAYDREAM
2 parts vodka
2 parts DeKuyper Watermelon Pucker®
1 part triple sec
1 part orange juice
1 part half 'n half
Splash of grenadine
Shake with ice and strain into a shot glass.*
*Note: Because this recipe includes many ingredients,
it's easier to make in volume, about 6 shots.

D C
1 part Irish cream
1 part tequila
Layer in a shot glass.

DC-3

1 part sambuca
1 part Irish cream
1 part white crème de cacao
Layer in a shot glass.

DC-9

1 part sambuca
1 part rum cream liqueur
1 part coffee liqueur
Layer in a shot glass.

D-DAY

1 part 151-proof rum
1 part citrus vodka
1 part crème de banana
1 part raspberry schnapps
1 part orange juice
Shake with ice and strain into a shot glass.*

*Note: Because this recipe includes many ingredients,
it's easier to make in volume, about 6 shots.

DEAD BIRD

1 part Jägermeister®
1 part Wild Turkey®
Pour ingredients into a glass neat
(do not chill).

DEAD DOG
1 part bourbon
1 part beer
3 dashes of hot sauce
Layer in a shot glass.

DEAD END
1 part amaretto
1 part coffee liqueur
1 part grain alcohol
1 part Irish cream
Shake with ice and strain into a shot glass.

DEAD FROG 1
1 part coffee liqueur
1 part Irish cream
1 part green crème de menthe
Shake with ice and strain into a shot glass.

DEAD FROG 2

1 part melon liqueur
1 part Irish cream
Splash of grenadine
Shake with ice and strain into a shot glass.

DEAD FROG 3

1 part vodka
1 part 100-proof peppermint schnapps
1 part coffee liqueur
1 part green crème de menthe
1 part Irish cream
Shake with ice and strain into a shot glass.

DEAD MAN WALKING
2 parts vodka
2 parts Crown Royal® bourbon
1 part cola
Dash of lemonade
Shake with ice and strain into a shot glass.

DEATH BY FIRE
1 part peppermint schnapps
1 part cinnamon schnapps
1 part hot sauce
Shake with ice and strain into a shot glass.

DEATH BY SEX

1 part vodka
1 part Southern Comfort®
1 part amaretto
1 part sloe gin
1 part triple sec
1 part peach schnapps
Splash of orange juice
Splash of cranberry juice cocktail
Shake with ice and strain into a shot glass.*

*Note: Because this recipe includes many ingredients,
it's easier to make in volume, about 6 shots.

DEATH FROM WITHIN

1 part light rum
1 part dark rum
1 part vodka
Shake with ice and strain into a shot glass.

DEATH ROW
1 part whiskey
1 part 151-proof rum
Shake with ice and strain into a shot glass.

DEATH WISH 1
1 part Wild Turkey 101®
1 part 100-proof peppermint schnapps
1 part Jägermeister®
Shake with ice and strain into a shot glass.

DEATH WISH 2
1 part Wild Turkey®
1 part dark rum
1 part peppermint schnapps
1 part grenadine
Shake with ice and strain into a shot glass.

DECADENCE
1 part coffee liqueur
1 part Frangelico®
1 part Irish cream
Layer in a shot glass.

DECKCHAIR
1 part Southern Comfort®
1 part crème de banana
1 part orange juice
Shake with ice and strain into a shot glass.

DEEP BLUE SOMETHING
2 parts blue curaçao
1 part peach schnapps
1 part sweet and sour mix
Splash of lemonade
Splash of pineapple juice
Shake with ice and strain into a shot glass.

DEER SPERM
1 part Jägermeister®
1 part Irish cream
Shake with ice and strain into a shot glass.

DEMON DROP
1 part grain alcohol
1 part orange juice
Layer in a shot glass.

DEMON KNIGHT, THE
1 part peppermint schnapps
1 part vodka
1 part Hawaiian Punch®
Shake with ice and strain into a shot glass.

DEPTH CHARGE

1 shot glass of peppermint schnapps
12 ounces of beer (1)
Pour the schnapps into a shot glass. Pour
the beer into a large beer mug. Drop the
shot glass into the middle of the beer.
Drink it before it foams over.

DESERT SKIES

1 part apricot brandy
1 part rum cream liqueur
1 part coffee liqueur
Layer in a shot glass.

DEVASTATING BODY ROCKER

1 part blackberry brandy
1 part gin
Shake with ice and strain into a shot glass.

DEVIL YOU DON'T KNOW, THE
1 part chocolate liqueur
1 part Jägermeister®
Layer in a shot glass.

DEVIL'S KISS
1 part dark rum
1 part coffee liqueur
Splash of triple sec
Shake with ice and strain into a shot glass.

DEVIL'S MOUTHWASH
1 part black sambuca
1 part Southern Comfort®
Shake with ice and strain into a shot glass.

DEVIL'S PISS

2 parts grain alcohol
1 part frozen lemonade concentrate
1 part water
Shake with ice and strain into a shot glass.*
Note: This recipe is easier to make in volume, about 6 shots.

DIABLILLO, EL

2 parts tequila silver
1 part crème de cassis
Shake with ice and strain into a shot glass.

DIABLO

2 parts rum
1 part hot sauce
Layer in a shot glass.

DIAMOND CUTTER
1 part 151-proof rum
1 part 181-proof rum
1 part grenadine
Pour ingredients into a glass neat
(do not chill).
Chase immediately with anything.

DICK WELLS
2 parts Irish cream
1 part bourbon
Layer in a shot glass.

DICKIE TOE CHEESE
1 part blue curaçao
1 part vodka
Shake with ice and strain into a shot glass.

DIE HARD

1 part gold rum
1 part cinnamon schnapps
1 part citrus vodka
1 part whiskey
1 part tequila gold
1 part gin
Splash of banana juice
Splash of milk

Shake with ice and strain into a shot glass.*

*Note: Because this recipe includes many ingredients,
it's easier to make in volume, about 6 shots.

DIESEL FUEL

1 part spiced rum
1 part Jägermeister®

Shake with ice and strain into a shot glass.

DILDO BASHERS
3 parts sambuca
1 part Irish cream
Layer in a shot glass.

DIRTIEST ERNIE
1 part 151-proof rum
1 part grain alcohol
1 part 100-proof peppermint schnapps
Shake with ice and strain into a shot glass.

DIRTY DIAPER
1 part vodka
1 part amaretto
1 part Southern Comfort®
1 part melon liqueur
1 part raspberry liqueur
1 part orange juice
Shake with ice and strain into a shot glass.*
*Note: Because this recipe includes many ingredients,
it's easier to make in volume, about 6 shots.

DIRTY GIRL SCOUT COOKIE
1 part coffee liqueur
1 part Irish cream
1 part crème de menthe
Layer in a shot glass.

DIRTY LEPRECHAUN, THE
1 part Jägermeister®
1 part Irish cream
1 part melon liqueur
Layer in a shot glass.

DIRTY NAVEL
1 part white crème de cacao
1 part triple sec
Shake with ice and strain into a shot glass.

DIRTY NIPPLE
1 part sambuca
1 part Irish cream
Layer in a shot glass.

DIRTY OATMEAL
1 part Jägermeister®
1 part Irish cream
Layer in a shot glass.

DIRTY ORGASM
1 part triple sec
1 part Galliano®
1 part Irish cream
Layer in a shot glass.

DIRTY ROTTEN SCOUNDREL
1 part vodka
1 part melon liqueur
Pour ingredients into a glass neat
(do not chill).

DIZZY DAMAGE
1 part Jägermeister®
1 part 100-proof peppermint schnapps
1 part Goldschläger®
Shake with ice and strain into a shot glass.

D-NOBBIE
1 part rum
1 part sake
1 part vodka
Dash of hot sauce
Shake with ice and strain into a shot glass.

DO ME JUICE
1 part cinnamon schnapps
1 part peppermint schnapps
1 part 151-proof rum
1 part Jägermeister®
Shake with ice and strain into a shot glass.

DOCTOR PEPPER
1 shot glass of amaretto
½ glass of beer
Drop the shot glass of amaretto into the beer. Chug before it foams over.

DOLT BOLT
1 part grain alcohol
1 part 100-proof peppermint schnapps
1 part Goldschläger®
Pour ingredients into a glass neat
(do not chill).

DOMINATOR
1 part peppermint schnapps
1 part coffee liqueur
1 part triple sec
Shake with ice and strain into a shot glass.

DON QUIXOTE

1 part Guinness® stout
1 part tequila
Pour ingredients into a glass neat
(do not chill).

DONG

1 part Irish cream
1 part 100-proof peppermint schnapps
Shake with ice and strain into a shot glass.

DON'T TRUST ME

2 parts cinnamon schnapps
1 part butterscotch schnapps
1 part 151-proof rum
Layer in a shot glass.

DOOR COUNTY CHERRY CHEESECAKE
1 part vanilla schnapps
1 part maraschino cherry juice
1 part cranberry juice cocktail
Splash of cream
Shake with ice and strain into a shot glass.

DOUBLE BERRY BLAST
1 part blueberry schnapps
1 part strawberry schnapps
Shake with ice and strain into a shot glass.

DOUBLE GOLD
1 part Goldschläger®
1 part gold tequila
Layer in a shot glass.

DOUBLE HOMICIDE
1 part Jägermeister®
1 part Goldschläger®
1 part orange juice
Shake with ice and strain into a shot glass.

DOUBLE STRIKER
1 part rum
1 teaspoon frozen limeade concentrate
Shake with ice and strain into a shot glass.

DOUBLEMINT BLOWJOB
1 part coffee liqueur
1 part peppermint schnapps
Splash of cream
Shake with ice and strain into a shot glass.

DOUCET DEVIL
2 parts amaretto
1 part Southern Comfort®
1 part crème de banana
Layer in a shot glass.

DOWN IN ONE
2 parts vodka
1 part red curaçao
1 part gold rum
Pour ingredients into a glass neat
(do not chill).

DOWN THE STREET
1 part triple sec
1 part orange juice
1 part vodka
1 part raspberry liqueur
Shake with ice and strain into a shot glass.

DR. BANANA
1 part tequila
1 part crème de banana
Layer in a shot glass.

DR. J
1 part vanilla schnapps
1 part Jägermeister®
Shake with ice and strain into a shot glass.

DRAGON'S BREATH
1 part Firewater®
1 part 151-proof rum
Layer in a shot glass.

DRUNK IRISH MONK

1 part Irish cream
1 part Frangelico®
1 part brandy
Layer in a shot glass.

DRUNKEN GHOST

1 part peppermint schnapps
1 part tequila blanco
1 part ouzo
1 part vanilla ice cream
Shake with ice and strain into a shot glass.

DUBLIN DOUBLER

1 part Irish whiskey
1 part Irish cream
Shake with ice and strain into a shot glass.

DUCK FART
1 part coffee liqueur
1 part Irish cream
1 part Canadian whiskey
Layer in a shot glass.

DUCK'S ASS
1 part Irish cream
1 part coffee liqueur
1 part 151-proof rum
Shake with ice and strain into a shot glass.

DUKE'S NIGHTMARE
1 part whiskey
1 part tequila
Shake with ice and strain into a shot glass.

E.T.

1 part melon liqueur
1 part Irish cream
1 part vodka
Layer in a shot glass.

ETS

2 parts ponche crema
1 part crème de banana
1 part coconut rum
Shake with ice and strain into a shot glass.

EARTHQUAKE SHOOTER
1 part sambuca
1 part amaretto
1 part Southern Comfort®
Layer in a shot glass.

EASY DOES IT
1 part grain alcohol
1 part coffee liqueur
1 part Irish cream
Layer in a shot glass.

EDMONTON OILER
1 part pear flavored schnapps
1 part blue curaçao
Layer in a shot glass.

EH BOMB

1 part tequila
1 part crème de menthe
1 part ouzo
1 part Irish cream
Layer in a shot glass. After drinking say
"Eh!" like a Canuck.

ELECTRIC BANANA 1

1 part tequila
1 part banana liqueur
Layer in a shot glass.

ELECTRIC BANANA 2

1 part tequila
1 part crème de banana
1 part lime cordial
Layer in a shot glass.

ELECTRIC KAMIKAZE
1 part triple sec
1 part vodka
1 part blue curaçao
1 part lime juice
Shake with ice and strain into a shot glass.

ELECTRIC SCREWDRIVER
1 part Southern Comfort®
1 part amaretto
1 part orange juice
Shake with ice and strain into a shot glass.

ELECTRIC STORM
1 part Irish cream
1 part Goldschläger®
1 part Jägermeister®
1 part 100-proof peppermint schnapps
Shake with ice and strain into a shot glass.

ELECTRIC SURFBOARD
1 part blue curaçao
1 part pineapple juice
Dash of grenadine
Splash of lemon lime soda
Shake curaçao, pineapple juice, and grenadine with ice and strain into a shot glass. Top with a splash of lemon lime soda.

ELIPHINO
1 part sambuca
1 part triple sec
Layer in a shot glass.

ELVIS PRESLEY
1 part vodka
1 part Frangelico®
1 part crème de banana
1 part Irish cream
Shake with ice and strain into a shot glass.
Elvis loved peanut butter and
banana sandwiches.

EMBRYO
1 shot glass of peppermint schnapps
2 to 3 drops of half 'n half
Place 2 to 3 drops of half 'n half in the
center of a shot of chilled peppermint
schnapps.

EMERALD ROCKET
1 part coffee liqueur
1 part melon liqueur
1 part Irish cream
1 part vodka
Layer in a shot glass.

END OF THE WORLD, THE
1 part 151-proof rum
1 part Wild Turkey 101®
1 part vodka
Pour ingredients into a glass neat
(do not chill).

ENEBRIATOR

1 part amaretto
1 part gin
3 parts pineapple juice
1 part triple sec
1 part vodka

Shake with ice and strain into a shot glass.*

*Note: Because this recipe includes many ingredients,
it's easier to make in volume, about 6 shots.

ENOLA GAY

1 part Southern Comfort®
1 part 151-proof rum
1 part blue curaçao
1 part amaretto
1 part orange juice
1 part melon liqueur

Shake with ice and strain into a shot glass.*

*Note: Because this recipe includes many ingredients,
it's easier to make in volume, about 6 shots.

ERECT NIPPLE
1 part tequila blanco
1 part sambuca
Shake with ice and strain into a shot glass.

ESKIMO GREEN AND GOLD
1 part crème de menthe
1 part Golden Pear® liqueur
Layer in a shot glass.

ESKIMO JOE
1 part Irish cream
1 part crème de menthe
1 part cinnamon schnapps
1 part milk
Layer in a shot glass.

ESKIMO KISS

1 part amaretto
1 part cherry liqueur
Layer in a shot glass. Top with
whipped cream.

ESTONIAN FOREST FIRE

1 part vodka
2 drops of hot sauce
Slice of kiwifruit
Mix vodka and hot sauce in a shot glass.
Shoot. Eat the kiwi.

ESTRELLA DU SUR

2 parts orange flavored vodka
1 part peach schnapps
Shake with ice and strain into a shot glass.

EVERY CLOUD HAS A SILVER LINING
1 part blue curaçao
1 part kiwi liqueur
Dash of Irish cream
Layer curaçao and kiwi in a shot glass.
Place a dash of Irish cream in the center
to form the "cloud."

EXPLOSIVE
2 parts gold tequila
1 part triple sec
Shake with ice and strain into a shot glass.

EXTENDED JAIL SENTENCE
1 part whiskey
1 part Southern Comfort®
1 part tequila
Splash of pineapple juice
Shake with ice and strain into a shot glass.

EXTRATERRESTRIAL

1 part Irish cream
1 part melon liqueur
1 part vodka
Splash of 151-proof rum
Layer in a shot glass.

EYEBALL

Dash of grenadine
2 parts Irish cream
1 part blue curaçao
Layer in a shot glass.

F-16

1 part coffee liqueur
1 part Frangelico®
1 part Irish cream
Layer in a shot glass.

FACE OFF

1 part grenadine
1 part crème de menthe
1 part Marie Brissard Parfait Amour®
1 part sambuca
Layer in a shot glass.

FAHRENHEIT 5000
1 part Firewater®
1 part pepper-flavored vodka
3 dashes of hot sauce
Layer in a shot glass.

FALIX
2 parts dark rum
2 parts margarita mix
1 part lemon juice
Shake with ice and strain into a shot glass.

FANTASM

1 part lemon lime soda
1 part amaretto
1 part apple cider
1 part apple juice
1 part sour apple schnapps
Shake with ice and strain into a shot glass.*
*Note: Because this recipe includes many ingredients,
it's easier to make in volume, about 6 shots.

FAT BOX

1 part crème de banana
1 part blue curaçao
1 part coconut rum
1 part pineapple juice
Shake with ice and strain into a shot glass.

FAT CAT
2 parts Irish cream
1 part amaretto
1 part banana liqueur
Shake with ice and strain into a shot glass.

FEATHER DUSTER
1 part whiskey
Splash of blackberry brandy
Pour ingredients into a glass neat
(do not chill).

FIERY BALLS OF DEATH
1 part 151-proof rum
1 part grain alcohol
1 part triple sec
Shake with ice and strain into a shot glass.

FIERY BLUE MUSTANG
1 part banana liqueur
1 part blue curaçao
1 part grain alcohol
Shake with ice and strain into a shot glass.

FIERY KISS
1 shot cinnamon schnapps
Splash of clover honey
Shake with ice and strain into a shot glass.

FIFTH AVENUE 1
1 part brown crème de cacao
1 part apricot brandy
Splash of cream
Layer in a shot glass.

FIFTH AVENUE 2

1 part peppermint schnapps
1 part brandy
1 part brown crème de cacao
1 part triple sec
Layer in a shot glass.

FIG

2 parts coconut rum
1 part pineapple juice
1 part cranberry juice cocktail
Shake with ice and strain into a shot glass.

FIGHTIN' IRISH GOLD SHOT

1 part Irish cream
1 part Goldschläger®
Layer in a shot glass.

FIRE AND ICE 1
1 part cinnamon schnapps
1 part Irish cream
Layer in a shot glass.

FIRE AND ICE 2
1 part tequila
1 part peppermint schnapps
Shake with ice and strain into a shot glass.

FIRE IN THE HOLE
3 dashes of hot sauce
1 part ouzo
Cover the bottom of a shot glass with
hot sauce and fill with ouzo.

FIRE TRUCK
1 part Jägermeister®
1 part ginger ale
Chill Jägermeister and combine with ginger
ale in a shot glass.

FIREBALL
1 part coffee liqueur
1 part ouzo
Shake with ice and strain into a shot glass.

FIREBALL SHOOTER
1 part cinnamon schnapps
1 part 151-proof rum
2 dashes of hot sauce
Shake with ice and strain into a shot glass.

FISHERMAN'S WHARF
1 part triple sec
1 part Courvoisier®
1 part amaretto
Layer in a shot glass.

FIVE STAR GENERAL
1 part Jägermeister®
1 part 151-proof rum
1 part 100-proof peppermint schnapps
1 part Goldschläger®
1 part tequila
Shake with ice and strain into a shot glass.

FLAME THROWER
1 part white crème de cacao
1 part Benedictine®
1 part brandy
Layer in a shot glass.

FLAMING ARMADILLO
1 part tequila
1 part amaretto
Splash of 151-proof rum
Layer in a shot glass.

FLAMING BEE
1 part Barenjager®
1 part sambuca
Layer in a shot glass.

FLAMING BLAZER
1 part white crème de cacao
1 part Southern Comfort®
Splash of 151-proof rum
Float the 151-proof rum on top. Light the rum
with a lighter or match. Extinguish by placing
an empty shot glass over the shot. Always
extinguish the flame before consuming.

FLAMING BLUE
1 part anisette
1 part vermouth
Splash of 151-proof rum

Float the 151-proof rum on top. Light the rum
with a lighter or match. Extinguish by placing
an empty shot glass over the shot. Always
extinguish the flame before consuming.

FLAMING COCAINE
1 part cinnamon schnapps
1 part vodka
Dash of cranberry juice cocktail

Shake with ice and strain into a shot glass.

FLAMING COURAGE

1 part cinnamon schnapps
1 part peppermint schnapps
1 part melon liqueur
Splash of 151-proof rum

Float the 151-proof rum on top. Light the rum with a lighter or match. Extinguish by placing an empty shot glass over the shot. Always extinguish the flame before consuming.

FLAMING DIAMOND

1 part strawberry liqueur
1 part peppermint schnapps
1 part triple sec
Layer in a shot glass.

FLAMING DR. PEPPER
1 part amaretto
Splash of 151-proof rum
12 ounces of beer (1)

Fill a mug with beer. Fill a shot glass almost to top with amaretto. Float the 151-proof rum on top. Light the rum with a lighter or match. Extinguish by placing an empty shot glass over the shot. Always extinguish the flame before consuming. Drop the shot into the beer and drink before it foams over.

FLAMING DRAGON
1 part Green Chartreuse®
Splash of 151-proof rum

Float the 151-proof rum on top. Light the rum with a lighter or match. Extinguish by placing an empty shot glass over the shot. Always extinguish the flame before consuming.

FLAMING DRAGON SNOT

1 part crème de menthe
1 part Irish cream
Splash of 151-proof rum

Float the 151-proof rum on top. Light the rum
with a lighter or match. Extinguish by placing
an empty shot glass over the shot. Always
extinguish the flame before consuming.

FLAMING FART

1 part cinnamon schnapps
Splash of 151-proof rum

Float the 151-proof rum on top. Light the rum
with a lighter or match. Extinguish by placing
an empty shot glass over the shot. Always
extinguish the flame before consuming.

FLAMING FRUIT TREES
1 part peach schnapps
1 part banana liqueur
Splash of 151-proof rum
Float the 151-proof rum on top. Light the rum with a lighter or match. Extinguish by placing an empty shot glass over the shot. Always extinguish the flame before consuming.

FLAMING GLACIER
1 part cinnamon schnapps
Splash of 100-proof peppermint schnapps
Float the 100-proof schnapps on top. Light the schnapps with a lighter or match. Extinguish by placing an empty shot glass over the shot. Always extinguish the flame before consuming.

FLAMING GORILLA

1 part peppermint schnapps
1 part coffee liqueur
Splash of 151-proof rum

Float the 151-proof rum on top. Light the rum with a lighter or match. Extinguish by placing an empty shot glass over the shot. Always extinguish the flame before consuming.

FLAMING HURLEY

1 shot Southern Comfort®
Splash of Dr. Pepper®
Layer in a shot glass.

FLAMING ORGY

1 part grenadine
1 part crème de menthe
1 part brandy
1 part tequila
Layer in a shot glass.

FLAMING RASTA

1 part amaretto
1 part grenadine
Splash of 151-proof rum

Float the 151-proof rum on top. Light the rum
with a lighter or match. Extinguish by placing
an empty shot glass over the shot. Always
extinguish the flame before consuming.

FLAMING RUSSIAN

1 part vodka

Splash of 151-proof rum

Float the 151-proof rum on top. Light the rum with a lighter or match. Extinguish by placing an empty shot glass over the shot. Always extinguish the flame before consuming.

FLAMING SQUEEGE

1 part light rum

1 part vodka

1 part lemon juice

1 part limeade

1 part orange juice

Shake with ice and strain into a shot glass.*

Note: Because this recipe includes many ingredients, it's easier to make in volume, about 6 shots.

FLANDERS FLAKE-OUT
1 part sambuca
3 parts sarsaparilla
Pour ingredients into a glass neat
(do not chill).

FLAT TIRE
2 parts tequila
1 part black sambuca
Shake with ice and strain into a shot glass.

FLIRTING CARRIES
1 part triple sec
1 part peach schnapps
1 part strawberry liqueur
Layer in a shot glass.

FLOOZE BOOZE
1 part Jägermeister®
1 part root beer schnapps
Shake with ice and strain into a shot glass.

FLÜGEL
1 part cranberry-flavored vodka
1 part Red Bull® energy drink
Shake with ice and strain into a shot glass.

FLUKEMAN
1 part Irish cream
1 part melon liqueur
Layer in a shot glass.

FLYING MONKEY
1 part coffee liqueur
1 part banana liqueur
1 part Irish cream
Layer in a shot glass.

FOG

1 part vodka
1 part fresh lime juice
Shake with ice and strain into a shot glass.

FOKKER FRIENDSHIP

1 part peach schnapps
1 part crème de cassis
Shake with ice and strain into a shot glass.

FOUR FINE FRIENDS

1 part Jose Cuervo® tequila
1 part Jim Beam® Bourbon
1 part Jack Daniel's Whiskey®
1 part Johnny Walker® Red Label
Shake with ice and strain into a shot glass.

FOUR HORSEMEN 1
1 part Jägermeister®
1 part tequila
1 part sambuca
1 part light rum
Shake with ice and strain into a shot glass.

FOUR HORSEMEN 2
1 part whiskey
1 part sambuca
1 part Jägermeister®
1 part 100-proof peppermint schnapps
Pour ingredients into a glass neat
(do not chill).

FOURTH OF JULY 1
1 part blue curaçao
1 part vodka
1 part grenadine
Layer in a shot glass.

FOURTH OF JULY 2
1 part grenadine
1 part cream
1 part blue curaçao
Layer in a shot glass.

FOXY LADY
1 part cream
1 part amaretto
1 part crème de banana
Shake with ice and strain into a shot glass.

FREDDY KRUEGER
1 part sambuca
1 part Jägermeister®
1 part vodka
Shake with ice and strain into a shot glass.

FREEBASE
1 part coffee liqueur
1 part light rum
1 part dark rum
1 part ponche crema
Shake with ice and strain into a shot glass.

FREIGHT TRAIN
1 part tequila
1 part Irish cream
Layer in a shot glass.

FRENCH KISS

1 part amaretto
1 part white crème de cacao
1 part Irish cream
Layer in a shot glass.

FRENCH POUSSE-CAFÉ

1 part cognac
1 part grenadine
1 part maraschino liqueur
Layer in a shot glass.

FRENCH TOAST

1 part Irish cream
1 part cinnamon schnapps
1 part butterscotch schnapps
Shake with ice and strain into a shot glass.

FRENCH TRICOLOR

1 part blue curaçao
1 part orange curaçao
1 part sambuca
Layer in a shot glass.

FRONT BUMPER

1 part peppermint schnapps
1 part Southern Comfort®
Layer in a shot glass.

FROZEN BIRD

1 part Wild Turkey®
1 part 100-proof peppermint schnapps
Layer in a shot glass.

FRUIT LOOP

1 part amaretto
1 part blue curaçao
1 part grenadine
1 part milk

Shake with ice and strain into a shot glass.

FRUIT OF THE LOOM

1 part banana liqueur
1 part melon liqueur
1 part cherry brandy
1 part coconut rum

Shake with ice and strain into a shot glass.

FRUIT SALAD

1 part sour apple schnapps
1 part cherry schnapps
1 part grape schnapps
Splash of orange juice
Shake with ice and strain into a shot glass.

FRUIT TINGLES

1 part blue curaçao
1 part grenadine
Splash of lemonade
Shake with ice and strain into a shot glass.

FU2

1 part Goldschläger®
1 part melon liqueur
1 part 100-proof peppermint schnapps
1 part Jägermeister®
1 part 151-proof rum

Shake with ice and strain into a shot glass.*

Note: Because this recipe includes many ingredients,
it's easier to make in volume, about 6 shots.

FUCK ME UP

1 part coffee liqueur
1 part Irish cream
1 part banana liqueur

Shake with ice and strain into a shot glass.

FUNKY CHICKEN
1 part tequila
1 part Wild Turkey®
Pour ingredients into a glass neat
(do not chill).

FUQUA SPECIAL
1 part vodka
1 part coconut rum
Splash of pineapple juice
Splash of lemon lime soda
Shake with ice and strain into a shot glass.

FUTURE DANCE SQUAD
1 part vermouth
1 part sloe gin
Shake with ice and strain into a shot glass.

FUZZY AIDA
1 part peach schnapps
1 part grapefruit juice
Shake with ice and strain into a shot glass.

FUZZY BASTARD
1 part tequila
1 peppermint Altoid®
Place Altoid® in the bottom of a shot glass
and add tequila. Shoot tequila and then
chew the Altoid®.

FUZZY BLUE GOBBLER
1 part peach schnapps
1 part tropical schnapps
1 part Wild Turkey®
Shake with ice and strain into a shot glass.

FUZZY IRISHMAN
1 part raspberry liqueur
1 part butterscotch schnapps
1 part Irish cream
Layer in a shot glass.

FUZZY MEXICAN
1 part peach schnapps
1 part tequila
Shake with ice and strain into a shot glass.

FUZZY MONKEY
1 part vodka
1 part peach schnapps
1 part crème de banana
1 part orange juice
Shake with ice and strain into a shot glass.

FUZZY NAVEL

1 part vodka
1 part peach schnapps
1 part orange juice
Shake with ice and strain into a shot glass.

FUZZY NUTTED BANANA

1 part amaretto
1 part banana liqueur
Dash of grenadine
2 parts orange juice
Splash of peach schnapps
Shake with ice and strain into a shot glass.*

*Note: Because this recipe includes many ingredients,
it's easier to make in volume, about 6 shots.

FUZZY RUSSIAN
1 part vodka
1 part peach schnapps
Shake with ice and strain into a shot glass.

FUZZY SCREW SHOT
1 part vodka
1 part peach schnapps
1 part triple sec
Shake with ice and strain into a shot glass.

FUZZY SMURF
1 part blue curaçao
1 part apricot brandy
Shake with ice and strain into a shot glass.

G BOMB
1 part Goldschläger®
1 part vodka
Shake with ice and strain into a shot glass.

G SPOT
1 part Southern Comfort®
1 part raspberry liqueur
1 part orange juice
Shake with ice and strain into a shot glass.

G. T. O.

1 part vodka
1 part rum
1 part gin
1 part Southern Comfort®
1 part amaretto
1 part orange juice
1 part grenadine

Shake with ice and strain into a shot glass.*

Note: Because this recipe includes many ingredients,
it's easier to make in volume, about 6 shots.

G 4

1 part amaretto
1 part Irish cream

Layer in a shot glass.

GALACTIC ALE
1 part vodka
1 part blue curaçao
1 part blackberry liqueur
1 part lime juice
Shake with ice and strain into a shot glass.

GALAXY
1 part sambuca
5 drops of hot sauce
1 part tequila
Layer in a shot glass.

GANGBUSTER PUNCH
1 part vodka
1 part peach schnapps
1 part cranberry juice cocktail
Splash of lemon lime soda
Shake with ice and strain into a shot glass.

GANGREEN

1 part green crème de menthe
1 part Jägermeister®
1 part Irish cream
Shake with ice and strain into a shot glass.

GEIGERCOUNTER

1 part 151-proof rum
1 part Jägermeister®
Float the 151-proof rum on top. Light the rum
with a lighter or match. Extinguish by placing
an empty shot glass over the shot. Always
extinguish the flame before consuming.

GENETICALLY MANIPULATED
1 part rum
1 part Mandarin Napoleon® liqueur
1 part crème de banana
Dash of grenadine
1 part cream
Shake all but cream with ice and
strain into a shot glass.
Top with cream.

GENTLE BULL SHOT
1 part coffee liqueur
1 part gold tequila
1 part cream
Shake with ice and strain into a shot glass.

GERMAN BLOW JOB
1 part Irish cream
1 part Jägermeister®
1 part 100-proof peppermint schnapps
Layer in a shot glass.

GERMAN BURRITO
1 part tequila
1 part Jägermeister®
Shake with ice and strain into a shot glass.

GETAWAY CAR
1 part peach schnapps
1 part citrus-flavored vodka
Shake with ice and strain into a shot glass.

GHETTO BLASTER
1 part coffee liqueur
1 part Metaxa®
1 part tequila
1 part rye whiskey
Layer in a shot glass.

GHOSTBUSTER
1 part vodka
1 part melon liqueur
1 part pineapple juice
1 part orange juice
Shake with ice and strain into a shot glass.

GILA MONSTER
1 part orange juice
1 part Jägermeister®
1 part tequila
Layer in a shot glass.

GIN AND BEER IT
1 part gin
1 part beer
Pour ingredients into a glass neat
(do not chill).

GINGERBREAD
1 part Irish cream
1 part cinnamon schnapps
1 part butterscotch schnapps
Shake with ice and strain into a shot glass.

GIRL MOM WARNED YOU ABOUT, THE
1 part grenadine
1 part triple sec
1 part rum
1 part melon liqueur
1 part blue curaçao
Layer in a shot glass.

GIRL SCOUT COOKIE
1 part coffee liqueur
1 part milk
1 part 100-proof peppermint schnapps
Shake with ice and strain into a shot glass.

GLADIATOR
1 part amaretto
1 part Southern Comfort®
1 part orange juice
1 part lemon lime soda
Shake with ice and strain into a shot glass.

GLADIATOR'S STINGER
1 part brandy
1 part peppermint schnapps
1 part sambuca
Shake with ice and strain into a shot glass.

GLITTERBOX
1 part gold sambuca
1 part coffee liqueur
Shake with ice and strain into a shot glass.

GODFATHER
1 part amaretto
1 part scotch
Layer in a shot glass.

GODZILLA
1 part pepper-flavored vodka
1 part green crème de menthe
Shake with ice and strain into a shot glass.

GOLD BARON
1 part 100-proof peppermint schnapps
1 part Goldschläger®
Layer in a shot glass.

GOLD DIGGER
1 part whiskey
1 part Goldschläger®
Shake with ice and strain into a shot glass.

GOLD FURNACE
1 part Goldschläger®
2 dashes of hot sauce
Layer in a shot glass.

GOLD RUSH
1 part amaretto
1 part vodka
1 part Yukon Jack®
Layer in a shot glass.

GOLDEN COMFORT
1 part Goldschläger®
1 part Southern Comfort®
1 part Jägermeister®
Shake with ice and strain into a shot glass.

GOLDEN FLASH
1 part sambuca
1 part triple sec
1 part amaretto
Layer in a shot glass.

GOLDEN NIGHT
1 part amaretto
1 part Irish cream
1 part Frangelico®
Layer in a shot glass.

GOLDEN NIPPLE
1 part Goldschläger®
1 part butterscotch schnapps
Splash of Irish cream
Layer in a shot glass.

GOLDEN RUSSIAN
1 part vodka
1 part Galliano®
Shake with ice and strain into a shot glass.

GOLDEN T
1 part tequila
1 part amaretto
Layer in a shot glass.

GOOD 'N PLENTY
1 part sambuca
1 part tequila
Layer in a shot glass.

GOODY TWO SHOES

2 parts passion fruit liqueur
1 part blue curaçao
1 part pineapple juice
Shake with ice and strain into a shot glass.

GORILLA

1 shot 151-proof rum
1 shot Jägermeister®
Shake with ice and strain into a shot glass.

GORILLA FART 1

1 part light rum
1 part Wild Turkey®
Layer in a shot glass.

GORILLA FART 2

1 part 151-proof rum
1 part Southern Comfort®
1 part whiskey
Layer in a shot glass.

GORILLA SNOT 1

1 part port
1 part Irish cream
Layer in a shot glass.

GORILLA SNOT 2

1 part melon liqueur
1 part crème de banana
Splash of advocaat
Layer in a shot glass.

GORILLA SNOT 3
1 part Irish cream
1 part lime cordial
Layer in a shot glass.

GORILLA'S PUKE
1 part Wild Turkey 101®
1 part 151-proof rum
Layer in a shot glass.

GRAB MY COCONUTS
1 part gold rum
1 part coconut rum
1 part pineapple juice
Shake with ice and strain into a shot glass.

GRADUATE, THE

1 part amaretto
1 part Southern Comfort®
1 part pineapple juice
Layer in a shot glass.

GRAINSLIDE

1 part grain alcohol
2 parts Irish cream
2 parts coffee liqueur
Shake with ice and strain into a shot glass.

GRAND BAILEYS

1 part Baileys Irish Cream®
1 part triple sec
Layer in a shot glass.

GRAND SLAM

1 part crème de banana
1 part Irish cream
1 part triple sec
Layer in a shot glass.

GRANDMOM'S SLIPPER

1 part Irish cream
1 part vodka
Layer in a shot glass.

GRANDPA IS ALIVE

1 part amaretto
1 part vodka
Shake with ice and strain into a shot glass.

GRAPE CHILL

1 part grape schnapps
1 part lemonade
Splash of pineapple juice
Shake with ice and strain into a shot glass.

GRAPE CRUSH 1

1 part raspberry liqueur
1 part vodka
1 part blue curaçao
1 splash cranberry juice cocktail
Shake with ice and strain into a shot glass.

GRAPE CRUSH 2

1 part blue curaçao
1 part cranberry juice cocktail
1 part pineapple juice
1 part Southern Comfort®
1 part sweet and sour mix
1 part raspberry liqueur

Shake with ice and strain into a shot glass.*

Note: Because this recipe includes many ingredients,
it's easier to make in volume, about 6 shots.

GRAPEVINE SPECIAL

1 part brandy
1 part apricot brandy
1 part banana liqueur
1 part cherry liqueur
1 part triple sec

Shake with ice and strain into a shot glass.*

Note: Because this recipe includes many ingredients,
it's easier to make in volume, about 6 shots.

GRASSHOPPER SHOT
3 parts brandy
1 part blue curaçao
Shake with ice and strain into a shot glass.

GRAVE DIGGER 1
2 parts Irish cream
2 parts Jägermeister®
1 part 100-proof peppermint schnapps
Shake with ice and strain into a shot glass.

GRAVE DIGGER 2
1 part 151-proof rum
1 part Jim Beam®
Shake with ice and strain into a shot glass.

GREAT BALLS OF FIRE
1 part Goldschläger®
1 part cinnamon schnapps
1 part cherry brandy
Layer in a shot glass.

GREAT WHITE NORTH
1 part coffee liqueur
1 part Irish cream
1 part anisette
Layer in a shot glass.

GREAT WHITE SHARK
1 part whiskey
1 part tequila
Dash of hot sauce
Shake with ice and strain into a shot glass.

GREEK FIRE
1 part brandy
1 part ouzo
Shake with ice and strain into a shot glass.

GREEK LIGHTNING
1 part ouzo
1 part vodka
1 part raspberry liqueur
Shake with ice and strain into a shot glass.

GREEK REVOLUTION
1 part ouzo
1 part grenadine
Shake with ice and strain into a shot glass.

GREEK WAY, THE
1 part ouzo
1 part Metaxa®
Shake with ice and strain into a shot glass.

GREEN AFTERMATH
1 part 100-proof peppermint schnapps
1 part Mountain Dew®
Shake with ice and strain into a shot glass.

GREEN APPLE
1 part Southern Comfort®
Splash of melon liqueur
Splash of sour mix
Shake with ice and strain into a shot glass.

GREEN APPLE TOFFEE
1 part vodka
1 part butterscotch schnapps
1 part sour apple schnapps
Shake with ice and strain into a shot glass.

GREEN BEAVER
1 part white crème de cacao
1 part crème de menthe
1 part Irish cream
Layer in a shot glass.

GREEN BERET
1 part vodka
1 part green crème de menthe
Shake with ice and strain into a shot glass.

GREEN BOMBER

1 part melon liqueur
1 part lime juice
1 part sweet vermouth
1 part gin
1 part beer

Shake with ice and strain into a shot glass.*

*Note: Because this recipe includes many ingredients,
it's easier to make in volume, about 6 shots.

GREEN BOOGER

1 part Irish cream
1 part crème de menthe
Splash of lime juice

Shake with ice and strain into a shot glass.

GREEN COOKIE MONSTER
1 part gin
1 part melon liqueur
1 part light rum
Shake with ice and strain into a shot glass.

GREEN DINOSAUR
1 part vodka
1 part gin
1 part melon liqueur
Shake with ice and strain into a shot glass.

GREEN EMERALD
1 part crème de menthe
1 part amaretto
Layer in a shot glass.

GREEN FLY SHOOTER
1 part green crème de menthe
1 part melon liqueur
Layer in a shot glass.

GREEN GECKO
1 part peppermint schnapps
1 part triple sec
1 splash limoncello
Shake with ice and strain into a shot glass.

GREEN LIZARD
1 part Green Chartreuse®
1 part 151-proof rum
Shake with ice and strain into a shot glass.

GREEN LIZARD ON THE BEACH

1 part crème de banana
1 part blue curaçao
Splash of orange juice
Shake with ice and strain into a shot glass.

GREEN MONKEY

1 part banana liqueur
1 part crème de menthe
Layer in a shot glass.

GREEN MONSTER, THE

1 part Cointreau®
1 part melon liqueur
1 part peach schnapps
1 part Southern Comfort®
1 part vodka
Shake with ice and strain into a shot glass.*

*Note: Because this recipe contains many ingredients,
it's easier to make in volume, about 6 shots.

GREEN SNEAKER
1 part vodka
1 part melon liqueur
1 part Cointreau®
Splash of cream
Shake with ice and strain into a shot glass.

GREEN SPIDER
1 part vodka
1 part green crème de menthe
Shake with ice and strain into a shot glass.

GREEN WITH ENVY
1 part green crème de menthe
1 part sambuca
Splash of Irish cream
Layer in a shot glass.

GREEN-EYED BLONDE

1 part melon liqueur
1 part banana liqueur
1 part Irish cream
Layer in a shot glass.

GRENADE

1 part vodka
1 part triple sec
1 part grenadine
Shake with ice and strain into a shot glass.

GREYHOUND

1 part Cointreau®
1 part Drambuie®
Shake with ice and strain into a shot glass.

GROSS ONE

1 part amaretto
1 part gin
1 part whiskey
1 part sambuca
1 part vodka

Shake with ice and strain into a shot glass.*

*Note: Because this recipe includes many ingredients, it's easier to make in volume, about 6 shots.

GSM

1 part gin
1 teaspoon sugar
1 part milk

Shake with ice and strain into a shot glass.

GUILLOTINE

2 parts butterscotch schnapps
1 part Irish cream
1 part cinnamon schnapps
Layer in a shot glass.

GUMBALL HUMMER

1 part raspberry schnapps
1 part banana liqueur
1 part grapefruit juice
Shake with ice and strain into a shot glass.

GUMBALL SHOOTER

1 part blue curaçao
1 part sambuca
Shake with ice and strain into a shot glass.

HALLOWEEN SHOOTER
1 part Licor 43®
1 part sambuca
Shake with ice and strain into a shot glass.

HAND GRENADE 1
1 part vodka
1 part Mountain Dew®
1 part pineapple juice
Shake with ice and strain into a shot glass.

HAND GRENADE 2
1 part Jägermeister®
1 part 100-proof peppermint schnapps
1 part 151-proof rum
Shake with ice and strain into a shot glass.

HANGIN' AROUND
1 part tequila blanco
1 part triple sec
1 part grenadine
Shake with ice and strain into a shot glass.

HAPPY JUICE
1 part lemon juice
1 part vodka
Shake with ice and strain into a shot glass.

HAPPY TOOTH
1 part coffee liqueur
1 part sambuca
Shake with ice and strain into a shot glass.

HARBOR LIGHTS 1
1 part coffee liqueur
1 part Irish cream
Splash of 151-proof rum
Shake with ice and strain into a shot glass.
Top with 151-proof rum.

HARBOR LIGHTS 2
1 part crème de menthe
1 part peppermint schnapps
1 part Irish cream
1 part triple sec
Layer in a shot glass.

HARD BEDROCK, A
1 part sambuca
1 part coffee liqueur
Shake with ice and strain into a shot glass.

HARD ROCKA
1 part melon liqueur
1 part vodka
1 part Irish cream
Layer in a shot glass.

HARD-ON
1 part coffee liqueur
1 part amaretto
1 part Irish cream
Layer in a shot glass.

HARLEY DAVIDSON 1
1 part Irish cream
1 part melon liqueur
1 part Jägermeister®
Shake with ice and strain into a shot glass.

HARLEY DAVIDSON 2
1 part Yukon Jack®
1 part whiskey
Shake with ice and strain into a shot glass.

HAWAIIAN PUNCH
1 part Southern Comfort®
1 part sloe gin
1 part orange juice
1 part amaretto
Shake with ice and strain into a shot glass.

HAWAIIAN PUNCH FROM HELL

1 part vodka
1 part Southern Comfort®
1 part amaretto
Splash of orange juice
Splash of lemon lime soda
Splash of grenadine
Shake with ice and strain into a shot glass.*
*Note: Because this recipe includes many ingredients,
it's easier to make in volume, about 6 shots.

HAWAIIAN PUNCH OUT

1 part light rum
1 part Hawaiian Punch®
Shake with ice and a strain into a shot glass.

HAZELNUT CHILL
1 part Frangelico®
1 part lemonade
1 part pineapple juice
Shake with ice and a strain into a shot glass.

HEAD IN THE SAND
1 part peppermint schnapps
1 part brandy
1 part tequila blanco
1 part grenadine
Shake with ice and strain into a shot glass.

HEAD ROOM
1 part crème de banana
1 part melon liqueur
Shake with ice and strain into a shot glass.

HEAD RUSH

1 part peach schnapps
1 part pear liqueur
1 part sambuca
Shake with ice and strain into a shot glass.

HEART ATTACK

1 part ginger liqueur
1 part melon liqueur
Splash of grenadine
Shake with ice and strain into a shot glass.

HEARTBREAKER

1 part amaretto
1 part Irish cream
1 part peach schnapps
Layer in a shot glass.

HEAVENLY BODY
1 part pear-flavored liqueur
1 part Frangelico®
1 part Irish cream
Layer in a shot glass.

HEILIG
1 part blueberry schnapps
1 part vodka
Splash of cranberry juice cocktail
Layer in a shot glass.

HELICOPTER
1 part Green Chartreuse®
1 part 151-proof rum
Layer in a shot glass.

HELLFIRE

3 parts rye whiskey
1 part hot sauce
Layer in a shot glass.

HELLRAISER

1 part melon liqueur
1 part black sambuca
1 part strawberry liqueur
Shake with ice and strain into a shot glass.

HELL'S GATE

1 part brandy
1 part butterscotch schnapps
Splash of hot sauce
Pinch of wasabi
Layer in a shot glass.

HEROIN

1 part black sambuca
1 part triple sec
Shake with ice and strain into a shot glass.

HIALEAH HOOKER

1 part strawberry liqueur
1 part Courvoisier®
1 part vodka
1 part rum
Shake with ice and strain into a shot glass.

HIT AND RUN

1 part anisette
1 part gin
Shake with ice and strain into a shot glass.

HOLE

1 part Irish cream
1 part light rum
1 part vodka
Shake with ice and strain into a shot glass.

HOLE-IN-ONE SHOOTER

1 part melon liqueur
1 part apple brandy
2 dashes of half 'n half
Shake with ice and strain into a shot glass.

HONEY BEAR

1 part cream
1 part coffee liqueur
1 part Frangelico®
1 part honey
Shake with ice and strain into a shot glass.

HONEY GETTER
1 part gin
1 part cranberry juice cocktail
1 part orange juice
Shake with ice and strain into a shot glass.

HONEY-DEW-ME
2 parts Bärenjäger®
1 part melon liqueur
4 parts orange juice
Shake with ice and strain into a shot glass.

HONOLULU ACTION

1 part tequila
1 part vodka
1 part 151-proof rum
1 part melon liqueur
1 part blue curaçao
1 part Irish cream
1 part grenadine
Whipped cream

Shake with ice and strain into a shot glass.*

Note: Because this recipe includes many ingredients,
it's easier to make in volume, about 6 shots.

HONOLULU HAMMER SHOOTER

2 parts vodka
1 part amaretto
1 part pineapple juice

Shake with ice and strain into a shot glass.

HORNY BASTARD
1 part vodka
1 part caramel liqueur
Splash of grenadine
Shake with ice and strain into a shot glass.

HORNY BULL 1
1 part tequila
1 part rum
Pour ingredients into a glass neat
(do not chill).

HORNY BULL 2
1 part tequila
1 part Southern Comfort®
Pour ingredients into a glass neat
(do not chill).

HORNY BULL 3

1 part tequila
1 part light rum
1 part Smirnoff® vodka
Pour ingredients into a glass neat
(do not chill).

HORNY GIRL SCOUT

1 part coffee liqueur
1 part peppermint schnapps
Pour ingredients into a glass neat
(do not chill).

HORNY MOHICAN

1 part banana liqueur
1 part Irish cream
1 part coconut rum
Pour ingredients into a glass neat
(do not chill).

HORNY SOUTHERNER
1 part Southern Comfort®
1 part melon liqueur
1 part sweet and sour mix
1 part lemon lime soda
Shake with ice and strain into a shot glass.

HOT AFTERNOON
1 part peach schnapps
1 part coffee liqueur
Shake with ice and strain into a shot glass.

HOT APPLE PIE
1 part Irish cream
1 part Goldschläger®
Dash of cinnamon
Shake with ice and strain into a shot glass.

HOT BEACH SHOOTER
1 part hot coffee
1 part peach schnapps
1 part coconut rum
Shake with ice and strain into a shot glass.

HOT BITCH
1 part vodka
1 part whiskey
1 part gin
Dash of hot sauce
Pour ingredients into a glass neat
(do not chill).

HOT BROWN LIZARD
1 part cinnamon schnapps
1 part melon liqueur
Pour ingredients into a glass neat
(do not chill).

HOT DAMN
1 part whiskey
1 part rum
1 part vodka
1 part orange juice
Shake with ice and strain into a shot glass.

HOT DECK SHOOTER
1 part whiskey
1 part sweet vermouth
1 part ginger ale
Shake with ice and strain into a shot glass.

HOT JIZZ
1 part melon liqueur
1 part cinnamon schnapps
1 part grain alcohol
1 part lemon lime soda
Layer in a shot glass.

HOT PANTS
1 part peach schnapps
1 part pepper-flavored vodka
Shake with ice and strain into a shot glass.

HOT SEX
1 part hot chocolate
1 part ginger liqueur
Layer in a shot glass.

HOT SHIT
1 part cinnamon schnapps
Splash of hot sauce
Dash of barbecue sauce
Layer in a shot glass.

HOT SHOT SHOOTER
1 part hot coffee
1 part cream
Layer in a shot glass.

HOT SPOT
1 part vodka
1 part tequila
1 part hot sauce
Layer in a shot glass.

HOT TO TROT
1 part cinnamon schnapps
1 part tequila
Dash of lime juice
Layer in a shot glass.

HOWLING COYOTE
1 part Chambord®
3 parts tequila
Shake with ice and strain into a shot glass.

HUNGER STRIKE
1 part peppermint liqueur
1 part coffee liqueur
Shake with ice and strain into a shot glass.

HURRICANE HUGO

1 part vodka
1 part amaretto
1 part sloe gin
Splash of melon liqueur
Splash of Southern Comfort®
1 part orange juice
1 part cranberry juice cocktail
Shake with ice and strain into shot glass.*
*Note: Because this recipe includes many ingredients,
it's easier to make in volume, about 6 shots.

HURRICANE SHOOTER

1 part anisette
1 part blue curaçao
1 part tequila
1 part Irish cream
Layer in a shot glass.

ICE CAPS
1 part peppermint schnapps
1 part vodka
Shake with ice and strain into a shot glass.

ICE CREAM SHOT
1 part vanilla schnapps
1 part Irish cream
Shake with ice and strain into a shot glass.

ICED BLUES
1 part blackberry liqueur
1 part blue curaçao
Shake with ice and strain into a shot glass.

ICY AFTER EIGHT
1 part vodka
1 part chocolate syrup
1 part green crème de menthe
Shake with ice and strain into a shot glass.

IGUANA
1 part vodka
1 part tequila
1 part coffee liqueur
Shake with ice and strain into a shot glass.

ILLICIT AFFAIR
1 part Irish cream
1 part peppermint schnapps
Layer in a shot glass. Top with
whipped cream.

ILLUSION
1 part coconut rum
1 part melon liqueur
1 part vodka
1 part Cointreau®
Splash of pineapple juice
Shake with ice and strain into a shot glass.*
*Note: Because this recipe includes many ingredients,
it's easier to make in volume, about 6 shots.

IMMACULATE INGESTION
1 part coffee liqueur
1 part peppermint schnapps
1 part vodka
Shake with ice and strain into a shot glass.

IN THE NAVY
1 part white crème de cacao
1 part peppermint schnapps
Shake with ice and strain into a shot glass.

INHALER
1 part Courvoisier®
1 part amaretto
Layer in a shot glass.

INK SPOT
1 part blackberry schnapps
1 part peppermint schnapps
Layer in a shot glass.

INNOCENT EYES
1 part coffee liqueur
1 part sambuca
1 part Irish cream
Layer in a shot glass.

INTERNATIONAL INCIDENT
1 part vodka
1 part coffee liqueur
1 part amaretto
1 part Frangelico®
1 part Irish cream
Shake with ice and strain into a shot glass.

INTO THE BLUE

1 part blue curaçao
1 part pineapple juice
1 part coffee liqueur
Shake with ice and strain into a shot glass.

I.R.A.

1 part Irish cream
1 part Irish Mist®
1 part Irish whiskey
Shake with ice and strain into a shot glass.

IRISH BROGUE

1 part whiskey
1 part Irish Mist®
Shake with ice and strain into a shot glass.

IRISH CAR BOMB

Guinness® stout
1 part Irish whiskey
1 part coffee liqueur
1 part Irish cream

Fill a mug two-thirds full with Guinness® and a shot glass with the liqueurs. Drop the shot glass into the mug and chug it down. Try not to let the shot glass hit your teeth.

IRISH GOLD

1 part Irish cream
1 part Goldschläger®

Shake with ice and strain into a shot glass.

IRISH HEADLOCK
1 part brandy
1 part amaretto
1 part Irish whiskey
1 part Irish cream
Layer in a shot glass.

IRISH KISS
1 part Irish cream
1 part 100-proof peppermint schnapps
Layer in a shot glass.

IRISH MONK
1 part Frangelico®
1 part peppermint schnapps
1 part Irish cream
Layer in a shot glass.

IRISH MONKEY
1 part Irish cream
1 part crème de banana
Layer in a shot glass.

IRISH NUT
1 part Frangelico®
1 part Irish cream
Layer in a shot glass.

IRISH SETTER
1 part Irish Mist®
1 part Frangelico®
1 part peppermint schnapps
1 part brandy
Shake with ice and strain into a shot glass.

IRISH SLAMMER
1 part crème de banana
1 part whiskey
Shake with ice and strain into a shot glass.

IRISH SUNRISE
1 part amaretto
1 part banana liqueur
1 part Irish cream
Layer in a shot glass.

IRISH SUNSET
1 part banana liqueur
1 part amaretto
1 part Irish cream
Layer in a shot glass.

IRISH TRICOLOUR
1 part crème de banana
1 part Irish cream
1 part melon liqueur
Layer in a shot glass.

IRISH WIDOW
1 part Irish cream
1 part sambuca
Layer in a shot glass.

IRON CROSS
1 part peppermint schnapps
1 part apricot brandy
Layer in a shot glass.

IRON LUNG

1 part Yukon Jack®
Splash of 151-proof rum
Whipped cream
Layer in a shot glass.

IRONMAN

1 part Green Chartreuse®
1 part sambuca
1 part scotch
3 parts hot sauce
1 part tequila
Pour ingredients into a glass neat
(do not chill).

ITALIAN RUSSIAN
1 part vodka
1 part sambuca
Pour ingredients into a glass neat
(do not chill).

ITALIAN SPEAR
1 part peppermint schnapps
1 part amaretto
Shake with ice and strain into a shot glass.

ITALIAN STALLION
1 part sambuca
1 part amaretto
1 part Frangelico®
Shake with ice and strain into a shot glass.

ITALIAN STALLION SHOOTER
1 part cream
1 part crème de banana
Shake with ice and strain into a shot glass.

ITALIAN VALIUM
1 part vodka
1 part amaretto
Shake with ice and strain into a shot glass.

JACK-ASS

1 part cinnamon schnapps
1 part Yukon Jack®
Shake with ice and strain into a shot glass.

JACK-HAMMER

1 part whiskey
1 part tequila
Pour ingredients into a glass neat
(do not chill).

JACK IN THE BOX
1 part coffee liqueur
1 part Jack Daniel's® whiskey
1 part crème de banana
Shake with ice and strain into a shot glass.

JACK AND JILL
1 part whiskey
1 part root beer schnapps
Shake with ice and strain into a shot glass.

JACK VOIGT
1 part spiced rum
1 part amaretto
1 part crème de banana
Shake with ice and strain into a shot glass.

JACK YOUR MELON
1 part Mountain Dew®
1 part watermelon schnapps
1 part whiskey
Shake with ice and strain into a shot glass.

JAGER BARREL
1 part Jägermeister®
1 part root beer schnapps
1 part cola
Shake with ice and strain into a shot glass.

JAGER MINT
1 part Jägermeister®
1 part peppermint schnapps
Shake with ice and strain into a shot glass.

JAGER OATMEAL COOKIE
1 part Jägermeister®
1 part coffee liqueur
1 part Irish cream
1 part butterscotch schnapps
Shake with ice and strain into a shot glass.

JAGER SHAKE
1 part Jägermeister®
1 part white crème de cacao
Dash of half 'n half
Shake with ice and strain into a shot glass.

JAGERITA
1 part Jägermeister®
1 part tequila
1 part lime juice
Pour ingredients into a glass neat
(do not chill).

JAGERSHOCK

1 part cinnamon schnapps
1 part Jägermeister®
Pour ingredients into a glass neat
(do not chill).

JAMAICA DUST

1 part Southern Comfort®
1 part coffee liqueur
1 part pineapple juice
Shake with ice and strain into a shot glass.

JAMAICA KISS

1 part coffee liqueur
1 part light rum
1 part milk
Shake with ice and strain into a shot glass.

JAMAICA MULE SHOOTER
1 part light rum
1 part dark rum
1 part lime juice
1 part ginger liqueur
Shake with ice and strain into a shot glass.

JAMAICAN 10 SPEED
1 part banana liqueur
1 part Irish cream
1 part melon liqueur
1 part vodka
Shake with ice and strain into a shot glass.

JAMAICAN BOBSLED
1 part vodka
1 part banana liqueur
Shake with ice and strain into a shot glass.

JAMAICAN CABDRIVER

1 part coconut rum
1 part orange juice
1 part cranberry juice cocktail
Shake with ice and strain into a shot glass.

JAMAICAN DUST

1 part light rum
1 part coconut rum
1 part pineapple juice
Shake with ice and strain into a shot glass.

JAMAICAN DUST-BUSTER

1 part rum
1 part coffee liqueur
2 parts pineapple juice
Shake with ice and strain into a shot glass.

JAMBALAYA
1 part peach schnapps
1 part Southern Comfort®
1 part sweet and sour mix
Dash of grenadine
Shake with ice and strain into a shot glass.

JAMBOREE
1 part vodka
1 part raspberry schnapps
Splash of cranberry juice cocktail
Shake with ice and strain into a shot glass.

JEDI MIND PROBE
1 part Irish cream
1 part butterscotch schnapps
1 part Jägermeister®
Shake with ice and strain into a shot glass.

JELL-O SHOTS

1 package instant Jell-O®
(see flavor combinations)
1 cup hot water
1 cup liqueur (see flavor combinations)

Basic Recipe:

Dissolve Jell-O® in hot water. Add liqueur.
Pour into small (1 or 1 part) paper cups.
Serve after the Jell-O® has set.

Flavor Combinations:

CAPE CODS—cranberry Jell-O®/vodka
GIMLETS—lime Jell-O®/gin
LEMONHEADS—lemon Jell-O®/vodka
COCO BLUE—blue raspberry Jell-O®/
coconut rum
COCO ISLANDS—island pineapple Jell-O®/
coconut rum
MARGARITAS—lime Jell-O®/tequila
MELON SOURS—lime Jell-O®/melon liqueur

JELLY BEAN 1
1 part blackberry brandy
1 part peppermint schnapps
Shake with ice and strain into a shot glass.

JELLY BEAN 2
1 part sambuca
1 part tequila
Splash of grenadine
Shake with ice and strain into a shot glass.

JELLY BEAN 3
1 part sloe gin
1 part Pernod®
1 part Southern Comfort®
Shake with ice and strain into a shot glass.

JELLY BEAN 4

1 part sambuca
1 part Galliano®
1 part grenadine
Shake with ice and strain into a shot glass.

JELLY BEAN 5

1 part tequila
1 part grenadine
1 part amaretto
Shake with ice and strain into a shot glass.

JELLY BEAN 6

1 part blackberry brandy
1 part cola
1 part anisette
Shake with ice and strain into a shot glass.

JELLY BEAN 7

1 part amaretto
1 part blackberry
1 part Southern Comfort®
Shake with ice and strain into a shot glass.

JELLY FISH

1 part white crème de cacao
1 part amaretto
1 part Irish cream
2 dashes of grenadine
Layer in a shot glass. Top with grenadine.

JIM MORRISON

1 part whiskey
1 part Jim Beam®
1 part Wild Turkey®
1 part Seagrams 7® whiskey
Pour ingredients into a glass neat
(do not chill).

JOE COCKER

1 part amaretto
1 part Southern Comfort®
1 part Crown Royal® bourbon
1 part whiskey
Pour ingredients into a glass neat
(do not chill).

JOE HAZELWOOD
1 part 100-proof peppermint schnapps
1 part Jägermeister®
Layer in a shot glass.

JOHNNY ON THE BEACH
1 part vodka
1 part melon liqueur
1 part blackberry liqueur
1 part pineapple juice
1 part orange juice
1 part grapefruit juice
1 part cranberry juice cocktail
Shake with ice and strain into a shot glass.*
*Note: Because this recipe includes many ingredients,
it's easier to make in volume, about 6 shots.

JOLLY RANCHER 1

1 part sweet and sour mix
1 part melon liqueur
Shake with ice and strain into a shot glass.

JOLLY RANCHER 2

1 part peach schnapps
1 part melon liqueur
1 part vodka
Shake with ice and strain into a shot glass.

JOSE FLAME-O

1 part Jose Cuervo® tequila
1 part Firewater®
Layer in a shot glass.

JOY OF ALMOND, A

2 parts coffee liqueur
1 part amaretto
1 part crème de almond
Shake with ice and strain into a shot glass.

JUDGEMENT DAY

1 part coffee liqueur
1 part Jägermeister®
1 part 100-proof peppermint schnapps
1 part 151-proof rum
1 part grain alcohol
Shake with ice and strain into a shot glass.*
*Note: Because this recipe includes many ingredients,
it's easier to make in volume, about 6 shots.

JUICY FRUIT
1 part raspberry liqueur
1 part triple sec
1 part melon liqueur
Shake with ice and strain into a shot glass.

JUICY LIPS
1 part vodka
1 part crème de banana
1 part pineapple juice
Shake with ice and strain into a shot glass.

JUST SHOOT ME

1 part Jim Beam®
1 part Jack Daniel's® whiskey
1 part Johnny Walker Red Label®
1 part Jose Cuervo® tequila
1 part Jägermeister®
1 part 151-proof rum

Shake with ice and strain into a shot glass.*

*Note: Because this recipe includes many ingredients,
it's easier to make in volume, about 6 shots.

KAISERMEISTER
1 part Jägermeister®
1 part root beer schnapps
Shake with ice and strain into a shot glass.

KAMIKAZE
1 part vodka
1 part triple sec
1 part lime juice
Shake with ice and strain into a shot glass.

KARTFART
1 part peppermint schnapps
1 part triple sec
1 part 151-proof rum
Shake with ice and strain into a shot glass.

KEY LIME PIE
1 part Licor 43®
1 part half 'n half
1 part lime juice
Shake with ice and strain into a shot glass.

KEY WEST SHOOTER
1 part vodka
1 part melon liqueur
Splash of orange juice
Splash of pineapple juice
Shake with ice and strain into a shot glass.

KILLER BEE

1 part Bärenjäger®
1 part Jägermeister®
Layer in a shot glass.

KILLER OREOS

1 part Jägermeister®
1 part coffee liqueur
1 part Irish cream
Shake with ice and strain into a shot glass.

KILLING SPREE

1 part passion fruit liqueur
1 part advocaat
Shake with ice and strain into a shot glass.

KILTED BLACK LEPRECHAUN

1 part Irish cream
1 part coconut rum
1 part Drambuie®
Layer in a shot glass.

KING'S RANSOM

1 part Goldschläger®
1 part Crown Royal® bourbon
Shake with ice and strain into a shot glass.

KISS OF DEATH

1 part Irish cream
1 part 151-proof rum
1 part 160-proof vodka
Layer in a shot glass.

KIWIKI

1 part vodka
1 part kiwi liqueur
1 part triple sec
Shake with ice and strain into a shot glass.

KLINGON DISRUPTER

1 part Jim Beam®
1 part mescal
1 part cinnamon schnapps
Shake with ice and strain into a shot glass.

KLONDIKE

1 part Irish cream
1 part Jägermeister®
Pour ingredients into a glass neat
(do not chill).

KNICK-KNACK
1 part advocaat
1 part whipped cream
1 part coffee liqueur
Layer in a shot glass.

KOKOPA
1 part peppermint schnapps
1 part coffee liqueur
Layer in a shot glass.

KOMY SHOT
1 part rum
1 part triple sec
1 part vodka
Splash of lemon juice
Shake with ice and strain into a shot glass.

KOOCH, THE
1 part cinnamon schnapps
1 part white crème de cacao
1 part Irish cream
Shake with ice and strain into a shot glass.

KOOL-AID
1 part vodka
1 part amaretto
1 part melon liqueur
1 part raspberry liqueur
Shake with ice and strain into a shot glass.

KOOL-AID (SOUTHERN STYLE)
1 part amaretto
1 part Southern Comfort®
1 part cranberry juice cocktail
Splash of grenadine
Shake with ice and strain into a shot glass.

KOOL-AID SHOT

1 part vodka
1 part amaretto
1 part sloe gin
1 part triple sec
Shake with ice and strain into a shot glass.

KRAZY KAT

1 part coffee liqueur
1 part crème de banana
1 part coconut liqueur
Shake with ice and strain into a shot glass.

KREMLIN SHOOTER

1 part vodka
Dash of grenadine
Shake with ice and strain into a shot glass.

KRIS KRINGLE

1 part crème de almond
1 part root beer schnapps
1 part half 'n half

Shake all ingredients but half 'n half with ice and strain into a shot glass. Layer half 'n half on top.

LADY KILLER (SHOOTER)
1 part coffee liqueur
1 part melon liqueur
1 part Frangelico®
Shake with ice and strain into a shot glass.

LAND MINE
1 part 151-proof rum
1 part Jägermeister®
Shake with ice and strain into a shot glass.

LAND ROVER

1 part dark crème de cacao
1 part dark rum
1 part spiced rum
1 part coffee liqueur
1 part Irish cream

Shake with ice and strain into a shot glass.*

*Note: Because this recipe includes many ingredients,
it's easier to make in volume, about 6 shots.

LANDSLIDE 1

1 part Irish cream
1 part apricot brandy
1 part banana liqueur
1 part coffee liqueur

Layer in a shot glass.

LANDSLIDE 2
1 part Irish cream
1 part triple sec
1 part amaretto
Layer in a shot glass.

LANDSLIDE 3
1 part amaretto
1 part crème de banana
Layer in a shot glass.

L.A.P.D. NIGHTSHIFT
1 part grenadine
1 part blue curaçao
1 part tequila
Layer in a shot glass.

LASER BEAM (SHOOTER)

2 parts Southern Comfort®
2 parts melon liqueur
1 part amaretto
1 part triple sec
2 parts pineapple juice
Shake with ice and strain into a shot glass.*
*Note: Because this recipe includes many ingredients,
it's easier to make in volume, about 6 shots.

LAST STOP, THE

1 part maraschino liqueur
1 part blackberry liqueur
Shake with ice and strain into a shot glass.

LATE BLOOMER

1 part triple sec
1 part apricot brandy
1 part rum
Layer in a shot glass.

LAVA

1 part Firewater®
1 part grain alcohol
Splash of hot sauce
Shake with ice and strain into a shot glass.

LAVA LAMP

1 part coffee liqueur
1 part strawberry liqueur
1 part Frangelico®
1 part Irish cream
3 drops of advocaat
Shake all ingredients but advocaat with
ice and strain into shot glass. Place the
advocaat in the center of the shot.*

*Note: Because this recipe includes many ingredients,
it's easier to make in volume, about 6 shots.

LAY DOWN AND SHUT UP!

1 part Jägermeister®
1 part cinnamon schnapps
1 part coffee liqueur
Splash of cream
Shake with ice and strain into a shot glass.

LAZER BEAM 1

1 part amaretto
1 part peach schnapps
Splash of orange juice
Shake with ice and strain into a shot glass.

LAZER BEAM 2

1 part anisette
Splash of grenadine
Shake with ice and strain into a shot glass.

LEATHER AND LACE 1
1 part amaretto
1 part peach schnapps
Layer in a shot glass.

LEATHER AND LACE 2
1 part coffee liqueur
1 part peppermint schnapps
1 part Irish cream
Layer in a shot glass.

LEATHER WHIP
1 part tequila
1 part triple sec
1 part whiskey
1 part peach schnapps
Shake with ice and strain into a shot glass.

LEMON DROP 1
1 part citrus vodka
1 lemon wedge
1 teaspoon sugar
Place the sugar on the lemon, take the shot
of vodka, and then suck on the lemon.

LEMON DROP 2
1 part spiced rum
1 lemon wedge
1 teaspoon sugar
Place the sugar on the lemon, take the shot
of rum, and then suck on the lemon.

LEMON LIGHTNING
1 part grain alcohol
1 part lemon juice
Shake with ice and strain into a shot glass.

LEMON MERINGUE
1 part vodka
Dash of lemon juice
Whipped cream
Shake with ice and strain into a shot glass.
Top with whipped cream.

LEPRECHAUN
1 part melon liqueur
1 part Irish whiskey
Shake with ice and strain into a shot glass.

LEPRECHAUN LYNCH
1 part Irish whiskey
1 part lime juice
Shake with ice and strain into a shot glass.

LEPRECHAUN SHOOTER
1 part blue curaçao
1 part peach schnapps
1 part orange juice
Shake with ice and strain into a shot glass.

LEPRECHAUN'S GOLD
1 part Irish cream
1 part Goldschläger®
Layer in a shot glass.

LET'S TANGO
1 part rum
1 part sambuca
1 part triple sec
Layer in a shot glass.

LEVITE PEPPER SLAMMER
1 part Southern Comfort®
1 part Dr. Pepper®
Pour ingredients into a glass neat
(do not chill).

LEWD LEWINSKY
1 part Jägermeister®
1 part cream
Layer in a shot glass.

LEWINSKY
1 part Irish cream
1 part Southern Comfort®
1 part peppermint schnapps
Shake with ice and strain into a shot glass.

LIBERACE

1 part coffee liqueur
1 part milk
1 part 151-proof rum

Layer in a shot glass. Float the 151-proof rum on top. Light the rum with a lighter or match. Extinguish by placing an empty shot glass over the shot. Always extinguish the flame before consuming.

LICORICE HEART

1 part strawberry liqueur
1 part sambuca
1 part Irish cream

Layer in a shot glass.

LIGHT HEADED
1 part blue curaçao
1 part coconut liqueur
1 part strawberry schnapps
Shake with ice and strain into a shot glass.

LIGHT-HOUSE
1 part coffee liqueur
1 part triple sec
1 part tequila
Layer in a shot glass.

LIL' SHEILA
1 part rum cream liqueur
1 part coffee liqueur
1 part peppermint schnapps
Shake with ice and strain into a shot glass.

LIME LIZARD
1 part vodka
1 part rum
1 part lime juice
1 part grenadine
Shake with ice and strain into a shot glass.

LIME-LIGHT
1 part vodka
1 part limoncello
Splash of lime juice
Shake with ice and strain into a shot glass.

LIPS
1 part tequila silver
1 part coffee liqueur
1 part grenadine
Shake with ice and strain into a shot glass.

LIQUID ASPHALT
1 part sambuca
1 part Jägermeister®
Layer in a shot glass.

LIQUID CANDY CANE 1
1 part vodka
1 part cherry liqueur
1 part peppermint schnapps
Layer in a shot glass.

LIQUID CANDY CANE 2
1 part cinnamon schnapps
1 part peppermint schnapps
Shake with ice and strain into a shot glass.

LIQUID COCAINE 1

1 part triple sec
1 part Southern Comfort®
1 part vodka
1 part amaretto
Splash of pineapple juice
Shake with ice and strain into a shot glass.

LIQUID COCAINE 2

1 part 100-proof peppermint schnapps
1 part Jägermeister®
1 part 151-proof rum
Shake with ice and strain into a shot glass.

LIQUID COCAINE 3

1 part tequila
1 part vodka
1 part gin
1 part light rum
1 part grain alcohol

Shake with ice and strain into a shot glass.*

Note: Because this recipe includes many ingredients,
it's easier to make in volume, about 6 shots.

LIQUID COCAINE 4

1 part vodka
1 part amaretto
1 part Southern Comfort®
1 part Cointreau®
1 part pineapple juice
Splash of lemon lime soda

Shake with ice and strain into a shot glass.*

Note: Because this recipe includes many ingredients,
it's easier to make in volume, about 6 shots.

LIQUID COCAINE 5

1 part rum
1 part 100-proof peppermint schnapps
1 part Jägermeister®
1 part Goldschläger®
Shake with ice and strain into a shot glass.

LIQUID COCAINE 6

1 part rum
1 part Jägermeister®
1 part root beer schnapps
1 part peppermint schnapps
Shake with ice and strain into a shot glass.

LIQUID COCAINE 8 BALL
1 part Southern Comfort®
1 part spiced rum
1 part amaretto
Splash of pineapple juice
Dash of grenadine
Shake with ice and strain into a shot glass.

LIQUID CRACK
1 part Jägermeister®
1 part 100-proof peppermint schnapps
1 part 151-proof rum
1 part Goldschläger®
Shake with ice and strain into a shot glass.

LIQUID HEROIN
1 part vodka
1 part 100-proof peppermint schnapps
1 part Jägermeister®
Shake with ice and strain into a shot glass.

LIQUID MENTOS
1 part blue curaçao
1 part peach schnapps
1 part banana liqueur
Shake with ice and strain into a shot glass.

LIQUID NITROGEN
1 part ouzo
1 part sambuca
Shake with ice and strain into a shot glass.

LIQUID QUAALUDE
1 part Jägermeister®
1 part Irish cream
Shake with ice and strain into a shot glass.

LIQUID VALIUM
1 part whiskey
1 part amaretto
1 part tequila
1 part triple sec
Shake with ice and strain into a shot glass.

LIT CITY
1 part Jägermeister®
1 part butterscotch schnapps
1 part Irish cream
Dash of Goldschläger®
Shake with ice and strain into a shot glass.

LITTLE BITCH

1 part Southern Comfort®
1 part amaretto
Splash of cranberry juice cocktail
Splash of orange juice
Shake with ice and strain into a shot glass.

LITTLE BLACK DEVIL

1 part crème de menthe
1 part light rum
Layer in a shot glass.

LITTLE NERVOUS, A
1 part vodka
1 part peach schnapps
1 part blackberry liqueur
Shake with ice and strain into a shot glass.
We had a band one night and at midnight
the bar was dead—the owner was losing
money–"he was just a little nervous."
by Kendra Tucker

LITTLE PIECE OF HELL, A
1 part 100-proof cinnamon schnapps
1 part sugar syrup
Pour ingredients into a glass neat
(do not chill).

LIZARD SLIME
1 part Jose Cuervo Mistico®
1 part melon liqueur
Layer in a shot glass.

LLOYD SPECIAL
1 part whiskey
1 part triple sec
Shake with ice and strain into a shot glass.

LOBOTOMY
1 part amaretto
1 part raspberry liqueur
1 part pineapple juice
Splash of champagne
Shake with ice and strain into a shot glass.
Top with champagne.

LONESTAR
1 part Marie Brissard Parfait Amour®
1 part cherry liqueur
1 part rum
Layer in a shot glass.

LOUD-MOUTH
2 parts Southern Comfort®
1 part peach schnapps
Shake with ice and strain into a shot glass.

LOUISIANA SHOOTER
1 piece raw oyster
1 part tequila
¼ teaspoon horseradish
Dash of hot sauce
Pour ingredients into a glass neat
(do not chill).

LOVE IS IN THE AIR
1 part amaretto
1 part crème de banana
1 part coconut liqueur
Shake with ice and strain into a shot glass.

LOVE ME TO DEATH
1 part scotch
1 part amaretto
Shake with ice and strain into a shot glass.

LOVELORN
1 part apricot brandy
1 part vermouth
Layer in a shot glass.

LUBE JOB

1 part vodka
1 part Irish cream
Layer in a shot glass.

LUI LUI

1 part vodka
1 part triple sec
1 part peach schnapps
Splash of sweet and sour mix
Splash of pineapple juice
Shake with ice and strain into a shot glass.*
*Note: Because this recipe includes many ingredients,
it's easier to make in volume, about 6 shots.

LUKSA'S APPLE PIE

1 part sour apple schnapps
1 part cinnamon schnapps
Splash of sweet and sour mix
Shake with ice and strain into a shot glass.

LUNA ROSSA

1 part peach schnapps
1 part Campari®
Splash of limoncello
Shake with ice and strain into a shot glass.

M & M

1 part Frangelico®
1 part white crème de cacao
Pour ingredients into a glass neat
(do not chill).

MACHINE SHOT

1 part 151-proof rum
Dash of Mountain Dew®
Layer in a shot glass.

MAD COW
1 part coffee liqueur
1 part cream
1 part 151-proof rum
Shake with ice and strain into a shot glass.

MAD HATTER
1 part vodka
1 part peach schnapps
1 part lemonade
1 part cola
Shake with ice and strain into a shot glass.

MAD MELON SHOOTER
1 part watermelon schnapps
1 part vodka
Layer in a shot glass.

MAD SCIENTIST

1 part blueberry schnapps
1 part raspberry schnapps
Splash of Irish cream
Layer in a shot glass.

MADMAN'S RETURN

1 part triple sec
1 part cinnamon schnapps
1 part cachaça
Shake with ice and strain into a shot glass.

MAGE'S FIRE

2 parts vodka
1 part cinnamon schnapps
1 part blue curaçao
Shake with ice and strain into a shot glass.

MAGGOTS
1 part vodka
1 part peach schnapps
Layer in a shot glass.

MAGIC POTION
1 part coffee liqueur
1 part amaretto
1 part dark crème de cacao
Shake with ice and strain into a shot glass.

MAIDEN'S PRAYER
1 part gin
1 part Lillet Blanc®
1 part apple brandy
Shake with ice and strain into a shot glass.

MALIBU COLA
1 part cola
1 part coconut rum
Pour ingredients into a glass neat
(do not chill).

MANCHURIAN CANDIDATE
1 part vodka
Dash of soy sauce
Add a dash of soy sauce to a shot of
chilled vodka.

MARIJUANA MILKSHAKE
1 part white crème de cacao
1 part melon liqueur
Splash of milk
Layer in a shot glass.

MARTIAN HARD-ON

1 part white crème de cacao
1 part melon liqueur
1 part Irish cream
Layer in a shot glass.

MASCONIVICH SHOOTER

1 part brandy
1 part triple sec
1 part cognac
Shake with ice and strain into shot glass.
Serve with a lemon wedge coated with sugar
on one side and instant coffee powder on the
other. Take the shot and bite the lemon.

MAX FACTOR

1 part raspberry liqueur
1 part cranberry juice cocktail
1 part triple sec
Shake with ice and strain into a shot glass.

MAYBE LATER

1 part blue curaçao
1 part crème de menthe
1 part white crème de cacao
Layer in a shot glass.

MCTAVISH

1 part scotch
1 part Irish cream
1 part butterscotch schnapps
Shake with ice and strain into a shot glass.

MEAT AND POTATOES
1 part vodka (potato)
1 slice of pepperoni
Chill potato-based vodka and garnish
with a slice of pepperoni.

MELARETTO
1 part melon liqueur
1 part amaretto
Shake with ice and strain into a shot glass.

MELLOW YELLOW
1 part Southern Comfort®
1 part Galliano®
Shake with ice and strain into a shot glass.

MELON BALL
1 part vodka
1 part melon liqueur
1 part pineapple juice
Shake with ice and strain into a shot glass.

MELON JONES
1 part melon liqueur
1 part grain alcohol
1 part sweet and sour mix
Shake with ice and strain into a shot glass.

MELONCHOLY BABY
1 part melon liqueur
1 part vodka
1 part triple sec
Shake with ice and strain into a shot glass.

MELONOMA

1 part vodka
1 part melon liqueur
Shake with ice and strain into a shot glass.

MEMORY LOSS

1 part banana liqueur
1 part vodka
1 part raspberry liqueur
1 part cranberry juice cocktail
1 part orange juice
Shake with ice and strain into a shot glass.*
*Note: Because this recipe includes many ingredients,
it's easier to make in volume, about 6 shots.

MENAGE À TROIS SHOOTER

1 part coffee liqueur
1 part Frangelico®
1 part triple sec
Layer in a shot glass.

MEXICAN BERRY
1 part coffee liqueur
1 part strawberry liqueur
1 part tequila
Layer in a shot glass.

MEXICAN BREEZE
1 part Irish cream
1 part Southern Comfort®
1 part tequila
Layer in a shot glass.

MEXICAN CHERRY
1 part tequila
1 part cherry liqueur
Layer in a shot glass.

MEXICAN CHICKEN
1 egg
1 part tequila
Dash of hot sauce
Layer in a shot glass.

MEXICAN FLAG
1 part grenadine
1 part crème de menthe
1 part tequila
Layer in a shot glass.

MEXICAN HORS D'OEUVRE
1 part tequila
1 jalapeño pepper
Splash of hot sauce
Layer in a shot glass.

MEXICAN INCA

1 part tequila blanco
1 part coffee liqueur
1 part grenadine
Layer in a shot glass.

MEXICAN LEPRECHAUN

1 part tequila
1 part crème de menthe
Shake with ice and strain into a shot glass.

MEXICAN PUMPER

1 part grenadine
1 part coffee liqueur
1 part tequila
Shake with ice and strain into a shot glass.

MEXICAN SNOWSHOE
1 part peppermint schnapps
1 part tequila
Layer in a shot glass.

MEXICAN THANKSGIVING
1 part tequila
1 part Wild Turkey®
Layer in a shot glass.

MIAMI ICE
1 part coconut rum
1 part coffee liqueur
Shake with ice and strain into a shot glass.

MIDNIGHT MADNESS

1 part triple sec
1 part coffee liqueur
1 part brandy
Shake with ice and strain into a shot glass.

MILD JIZZ

1 part melon liqueur
1 part coconut rum
1 part vodka
1 part lemon lime soda
Layer in a shot glass.

MILES OF SMILES

1 part amaretto
1 part peppermint schnapps
1 part rye whiskey
Layer in a shot glass.

MILK OF AMNESIA
1 part Jägermeister®
1 part Irish cream
Layer in a shot glass.

MILKY WAY 1
1 part amaretto
1 part dark crème de cacao
Layer in a shot glass.

MILKY WAY 2
1 part Tuaca®
1 part Irish cream
1 part coffee liqueur
Dash of cream
Shake with ice and strain into a shot glass.

MILKY WAY 3
1 part Irish cream
1 part root beer schnapps
1 part Goldschläger®
Shake with ice and strain into a shot glass.

MILWAUKEE RIVER
1 part blue curaçao
1 part coffee liqueur
Shake with ice and strain into a shot glass.

MIND COLLAPSE
1 part peppermint schnapps
1 part whiskey
Shake with ice and strain into a shot glass.

MIND ERASER

1 part coffee liqueur
1 part vodka
1 part tonic water
Layer on the rocks or in a double shot
glass filled with ice. Drink all at once
through a straw.

MIND PROBE

1 part 151-proof rum
1 part sambuca
1 part Jägermeister®
Shake with ice and strain into a shot glass.

MINI MARGARITA

1 part sweet and sour mix
1 part tequila blanco
1 part triple sec
Shake with ice and strain into a shot glass.

MINT CHOCOLATE
1 part green crème de menthe
1 part coffee liqueur
1 part Irish cream
Shake with ice and strain into a shot glass.

MINT JULEP SHOT
1 part bourbon
1 part green crème de menthe
Shake with ice and strain into a shot glass.

MINT SANDWICH
1 part amaretto
1 part white crème de cacao
1 part crème de menthe
Layer in a shot glass.

MINTARITA
1 part peppermint schnapps
1 part tequila blanco
Shake with ice and strain into a shot glass.

MISSING LINK
1 part peppermint schnapps
1 part sambuca
Shake with ice and strain into a shot glass.

MIXED MOCHA FRAPPÉ
1 part coffee liqueur
1 part crème de menthe
1 part white crème de cacao
1 part triple sec
Shake with ice and strain into a shot glass.

MODEL T
1 part coffee liqueur
1 part crème de banana
1 part amaretto
Layer in a shot glass.

MOM'S APPLE PIE
1 part sour apple schnapps
1 part cinnamon schnapps
Layer in a shot glass.

MONKEY'S PUNCH
1 part coffee liqueur
1 part crème de menthe
1 part Irish cream
Layer in a shot glass.

MONSOON

1 part amaretto
1 part coffee liqueur
1 part Frangelico®
1 part currant-flavored vodka
Shake with ice and strain into a shot glass.

MONTANA STUMP PULLER

1 part Canadian whiskey
1 part white crème de cacao
Shake with ice and strain into a shot glass.

MOOSE FART

1 part vodka
1 part Crown Royal® bourbon
1 part coffee liqueur
1 part Irish cream
Shake with ice and strain into a shot glass.

MORANGUITO
2 parts absinthe
2 parts tequila
1 part grenadine
Layer in a shot glass.

MORNING WOOD
1 part vodka
1 part peach schnapps
1 part orange juice
1 part sweet and sour mix
1 part raspberry liqueur
Shake with ice and strain into a shot glass.

MOTHER LOAD
1 part vodka
1 part blackberry liqueur
1 part coconut rum
Shake with ice and strain into a shot glass.

MOTHER PUCKER

1 part sour apple schnapps
1 part vodka
Splash of lemon lime soda
Splash of club soda
Shake with ice and strain into a shot glass.

MOTHER'S LOAD

1 part amaretto
1 part coffee liqueur
1 part light rum
1 part Southern Comfort®
Shake with ice and strain into a shot glass.

MOUTHWASH

1 part peppermint schnapps
1 part vodka
1 part blue curaçao
Shake with ice and strain into a shot glass.

MR. BEAN
1 part anisette
1 part blackberry liqueur
Shake with ice and strain into a shot glass.

MUD SLIDE
1 part vodka
1 part coffee liqueur
1 part Irish cream
Shake with ice and strain into a shot glass.

MUSHROOM
1 part grenadine
1 part Irish cream
1 part melon liqueur
Layer in a shot glass.

MUSSOLINI
1 part Goldschläger®
1 part Jägermeister®
1 part sambuca
Shake with ice and strain into a shot glass.

MUTATED MOTHER'S MILK
1 part Jägermeister®
1 part Irish cream
1 part peppermint schnapps
Shake with ice and strain into a shot glass.

NAKED GIRL SCOUT

1 part Godiva® liqueur
1 part 100-proof peppermint schnapps
Shake with ice and strain into a shot glass.

NAKED NAVEL

1 part vodka
1 part peach schnapps
Layer in a shot glass.

NAPALM

1 part Aftershock® cinnamon schnapps
1 part Fire and Ice®
Splash of 151-proof rum
Layer in a shot glass.

NAPALM-DEATH

1 part Cointreau®
1 part coffee liqueur
1 part Drambuie®
1 part Irish cream
Layer in a shot glass.

NASTY BITCH

1 part tequila
1 part Cointreau®
Shake with ice and strain into a shot glass.

NATURAL DISASTER
1 part cinnamon schnapps
1 part peppermint schnapps
Layer in a shot glass.

NAVY SEAL
1 part Crown Royal® bourbon
1 part spiced rum
Shake with ice and strain into a shot glass.

NECROPHILIAC
1 part blue curaçao
1 part advocaat
Layer in a shot glass.

NEON BULLFROG
1 part vodka
1 part blue curaçao
1 part melon liqueur
1 part sour mix
Shake with ice and strain into a shot glass.

NEON CACTUS
1 part cactus juice schnapps
1 part margarita mix
Shake with ice and strain into a shot glass.

NERD
1 part strawberry schnapps
1 part black sambuca
1 part cream
Shake with ice and strain into a shot glass.

NERO'S DELIGHT
1 part vodka
1 part sambuca
Shake with ice and strain into a shot glass.

NEURONIUM
1 part vodka
1 part peppermint schnapps
1 part cinnamon schnapps
Dash of grenadine
Shake all but grenadine with ice and strain
into a shot glass.
Top with grenadine.

NEVER A SEVEN
1 part whiskey
1 part tequila
1 part rum
1 part Goldschläger®
1 part hot sauce
Shake with ice and strain into a shot glass.

NEW ENGLAND KAMIKAZE
1 part triple sec
1 part sour mix
Shake with ice and strain into a shot glass.

NIGHT FLIGHT (TOURIST CLASS)
1 part amaretto
1 part peach schnapps
1 part blackberry liqueur
Shake with ice and strain into a shot glass.

NIGHT HAWK

1 part peppermint schnapps
1 part dark rum
Shake with ice and strain into a shot glass.

NINJA

1 part Frangelico®
1 part melon liqueur
Shake with ice and strain into a shot glass.

NIPPLE ON FIRE

1 part Firewater®
1 part butterscotch schnapps
1 part Irish cream
Layer in a shot glass.

NITRO

1 part sambuca
1 part Goldschläger®
1 part brandy
Shake with ice and strain into a shot glass.

NO CASH

1 part peppermint schnapps
1 part coffee liqueur
1 part Frangelico®
Shake with ice and strain into a shot glass.

NO NAME

1 part amaretto
1 part whiskey
1 part sour mix
Shake with ice and strain into a shot glass.

NORWEGIAN PASTRY

1 part dark crème de cacao
1 part coffee liqueur
1 part aquavit
1 part vanilla schnapps
Shake with ice and strain into a shot glass.

NUCLEAR ACCELERATOR

1 part peppermint schnapps
1 part citrus vodka
Shake with ice and strain into a shot glass.

NUCLEAR WASTE

1 part vodka
1 part melon liqueur
1 part triple sec
Dash of lime juice
Shake with ice and strain into a shot glass.

NUDE BOMB
1 part coffee liqueur
1 part amaretto
1 part crème de banana
Layer in a shot glass.

NUMERO UNO
1 part tequila blanco
1 part triple sec
Shake with ice and strain into a shot glass.

NUT-CRACKER
1 part vodka
1 part Frangelico®
1 part cream
Shake with ice and strain into a shot glass.

NUTHUGGER

1 part 151-proof rum
1 part vodka
1 part lime juice
Splash of beer
Layer in a shot glass.

NUTS 'N HOLLY

1 part Drambuie®
1 part Irish cream
1 part Frangelico®
1 part amaretto
Shake with ice and strain into a shot glass.

NUTS 'N NIPPLES

1 part Irish cream
1 part butterscotch schnapps
1 part Frangelico®
Shake with ice and strain into a shot glass.

NUTTY ARUBAN
1 part Frangelico®
1 part ponche crema
Shake with ice and strain into a shot glass.

NUTTY BUDDY
1 part Frangelico®
1 part amaretto
1 part peppermint schnapps
Shake with ice and strain into a shot glass.

NUTTY IRISHMAN
1 part Irish cream
1 part Frangelico®
Shake with ice and strain into a shot glass.

NUTTY JAMAICAN
1 part dark rum
1 part Frangelico®
Shake with ice and strain into a shot glass.

NUTTY MEXICAN
1 part tequila blanco
1 part Frangelico®
Shake with ice and strain into a shot glass.

NUTTY PROFESSOR 1
1 part triple sec
1 part Frangelico®
1 part Irish cream
Shake with ice and strain into a shot glass.

NUTTY PROFESSOR 2

1 part Mandarin Napoleon® liqueur
1 part Frangelico®
Shake with ice and strain into a shot glass.

NUTZ 'N BERRIES

2 parts Stolichnaya® lemon vodka
1 part Frangelico®
2 parts cranberry juice cocktail
Shake with ice and strain into a shot glass.

NYMPHOMANIAC

1 part spiced rum
1 part peach schnapps
1 part coconut rum
Shake with ice and strain into a shot glass.

OATMEAL COOKIE 1

1 part cinnamon schnapps
1 part Irish cream
Splash of coffee liqueur
Splash of Frangelico®
Splash of cream
Shake with ice and strain into a shot glass.*

Note: Because this recipe includes many ingredients,
it's easier to make in volume, about 6 shots.

OATMEAL COOKIE 2

1 part butterscotch schnapps
1 part Irish cream
1 part Goldschläger®
1 part Frangelico®
Shake with ice and strain into a shot glass.

OATMEAL COOKIE 3

1 part coffee liqueur
1 part Irish cream
1 part cinnamon schnapps
Shake with ice and strain into a shot glass.

OATMEAL COOKIE 4

1 part Jägermeister®
1 part cinnamon schnapps
1 part butterscotch schnapps
1 part Irish cream
Shake with ice and strain into a shot glass.

OATMEAL RAISIN COOKIE

1 part Jägermeister®
1 part Goldschläger®
1 part 151-proof rum
1 part coffee liqueur
1 part Irish cream

Shake with ice and strain into a shot glass.*

Note: Because this recipe includes many ingredients,
it's easier to make in volume, about 6 shots.

OCTOBER SKY

1 part vodka
1 part wild berry schnapps
1 part lemonade
1 part orange juice

Shake with ice and strain into a shot glass.

OFFER YOU CAN'T REFUSE, AN

1 part amaretto
1 part sambuca
Shake with ice and strain into a shot glass.

OH MY GOSH

1 part amaretto
1 part peach schnapps
Shake with ice and strain into a shot glass.

OH ZONE LAYER, THE

1 part triple sec
1 part sweet and sour mix
1 part blue curaçao
Layer in a shot glass.

OIL SLICK 1

1 part 100-proof peppermint schnapps
1 part Jägermeister®
Layer in a shot glass.

OIL SLICK 2

1 part 100-proof peppermint schnapps
1 part Jägermeister®
3 drops of blue curaçao
Layer in a shot glass.

OIL SLICK 3

1 part peppermint schnapps
1 part bourbon
Layer in a shot glass.

OKANAGAN

1 part apricot brandy
1 part strawberry liqueur
1 part blueberry schnapps
Layer in a shot glass.

OLD CRUSTY

1 part 151-proof rum
1 part Wild Turkey®
Pour ingredients into a glass neat
(do not chill).

OLD GLORY

1 part grenadine
1 part heavy cream
1 part Hypnotiq®
Layer in a shot glass.

OPEN GRAVE
1 part Jägermeister®
1 part 100-proof peppermint schnapps
1 part Irish cream
Shake with ice and strain into a shot glass.

OPERA HOUSE SPECIAL
1 part tequila
1 part gin
1 part light rum
1 part vodka
1 part pineapple juice
1 part orange juice
1 part sour mix
Shake with ice and strain into a shot glass.*

Note: Because this recipe includes many ingredients,
it's easier to make in volume, about 6 shots.

ORANGE CRUSH SHOOTER
1 part vodka
1 part triple sec
1 part soda water
Pour ingredients into a glass neat
(do not chill).

ORANGE MONK
1 part Frangelico®
1 part triple sec
Shake with ice and strain into a shot glass.

ORANGE VEST
1 part amaretto
1 part peach schnapps
Shake with ice and strain into a shot glass.

OREO COOKIE
1 part coffee liqueur
1 part white crème de cacao
1 part Irish cream
Splash of vodka
Layer in a shot glass.

ORGASM
1 part peppermint schnapps
1 part Irish cream
Shake with ice and strain into a shot glass.

ORGIES WITH A CHERRY
1 part vodka
1 part peach schnapps
1 part coconut cream
Dash of blue curaçao
Layer in a shot glass.

ORIGINAL TERMINATOR

1 part 100-proof peppermint schnapps
1 part black sambuca
Layer in a shot glass.

OTTER POP

1 part light rum
1 part blue curaçao
1 part sweet and sour mix
1 part lemon lime soda
Shake with ice and strain into a shot glass.

OXMIX
1 part blue curaçao
1 part ouzo
1 part lemon lime soda
Splash of black currant syrup
Layer in a shot glass.

OYSTER SHOT
1 oyster
1 part tequila
Dash of hot sauce
Layer in a shot glass.

PADDY'S DAY SPECIAL

1 part green crème de menthe
1 part triple sec
1 part melon liqueur
Shake with ice and strain into a shot glass.

PAINTBOX

1 part banana liqueur
1 part blue curaçao
1 part cherry liqueur
Layer in a shot glass.

PAIR O'CACKS
1 part vodka
1 part lemon juice
2 drops of hot sauce
Layer in a shot glass.

PAMOYO
1 part gin
1 part lemon lime soda
1 part grape juice
Shake with ice and strain into a shot glass.

PANCHO VILLA
1 part tequila blanco
1 part almond syrup
1 part 151-proof rum
Shake with ice and strain into a shot glass.

PANTHER

1 part peppermint schnapps
1 part peach schnapps
Shake with ice and strain into a shot glass.

PANTS ON FIRE

1 part banana liqueur
1 part grapefruit juice
1 part orange juice
1 part strawberry liqueur
1 part vodka
Shake with ice and strain into a shot glass.*

*Note: Because this recipe includes many ingredients,
it's easier to make in volume, about 6 shots.

PANTY BURNER SHOOTER

1 part advocaat
1 part coffee liqueur
1 part Frangelico®
Shake with ice and strain into a shot glass.

PANTY QUIVER
1 part Jägermeister®
1 part blackberry brandy
Shake with ice and strain into a shot glass.

PANTY RAID
1 part citrus vodka
1 part raspberry liqueur
Splash of lemon lime soda
Splash of pineapple juice
Shake with ice and strain into a shot glass.

PANTY SPLASH
1 part peach schnapps
1 part grenadine
1 part tequila gold
1 part 151-proof rum
Shake with ice and strain into a shot glass.

PAP SMEAR
1 part Pabst Blue Ribbon® beer
1 part Smirnoff® vodka
Pour ingredients into a glass neat
(do not chill).

PARALYZER
1 part coffee liqueur
1 part vodka
1 part cola
1 part milk
Shake with ice and strain into a shot glass.

PARANOIA
1 part amaretto
1 part orange juice
Shake with ice and strain into a shot glass.

PARROT HEAD
1 part blackberry liqueur
1 part dark rum
1 part spiced rum
1 part pineapple juice
Shake with ice and strain into a shot glass.

PARTY ANIMAL
1 part Parfait Amour®
1 part orange juice
1 part coconut liqueur
Shake with ice and strain into a shot glass.

PASADENA LADY
1 part amaretto
1 part brandy
Layer in a shot glass.

PASSED OUT NAKED
ON THE BATHROOM FLOOR

1 part 100-proof peppermint schnapps
1 part Jägermeister®
1 part tequila
1 part 151-proof rum
Shake with ice and strain into a shot glass.

PASSION CREAM

1 part white crème de cacao
1 part cream
Shake with ice and strain into a shot glass.

PASSION KILLER SHOOTER

1 part tequila blanco
1 part melon liqueur
1 part passion fruit liqueur
Shake with ice and strain into a shot glass.

PATRIOTIC BLOW
1 part sloe gin
1 part blue curaçao
Squirt of whipped cream
Layer in a shot glass.

PB&J 1
1 part vodka
1 part raspberry liqueur
1 part Frangelico®
Shake with ice and strain into a shot glass.

PB&J 2
1 part Frangelico®
1 part grenadine
Layer in a shot glass.

P. D. C.

1 part crème de menthe
2 parts black sambuca
2 parts Green Chartreuse®
1 part Irish cream
Layer in a shot glass.

PEACH NEHI

1 part vodka
1 part peach schnapps
1 part cherry schnapps
Splash of sour mix
Splash of pineapple juice
Splash of lemon lime soda
Shake with ice and strain into a shot glass.*

*Note: Because this recipe includes many ingredients,
it's easier to make in volume, about 6 shots.

PEACH PIRATE
1 part peach schnapps
1 part light rum
Shake with ice and strain into a shot glass.

PEACH SCHLAGER
1 part Goldschläger®
1 part peach schnapps
Splash of cranberry juice cocktail
Shake with ice and strain into a shot glass.

PEACH SMOOTHIE
1 part Yukon Jack®
1 part whiskey
1 part peach schnapps
Shake with ice and strain into a shot glass.

PEACH TART 1
1 part peach schnapps
1 part lime juice
Shake with ice and strain into a shot glass.

PEACH TART 2
1 part vodka
1 part peach schnapps
1 part DeKuyper Wilderberry® schnapps
Splash of sour mix
Shake with ice and strain into a shot glass.

PEARL DIVER
1 part melon liqueur
1 part pineapple juice
1 part coconut rum
Shake with ice and strain into a shot glass.

PEARL NECKLACE

1 part Tequila Rose®
1 part Irish cream
Shake with ice and strain into a shot glass.

PECKER WRECKER

1 part blackberry brandy
1 part creme de noyaux
1 part 151-proof rum
1 part pineapple juice
1 part cranberry juice cocktail
Shake with ice and strain into a shot glass.*
Note: Because this recipe includes many ingredients,
it's easier to make in volume, about 6 shots.

PECKERHEAD

1 part Southern Comfort®
1 part amaretto
1 part pineapple juice
Shake with ice and strain into a shot glass.

PEE GEE

1 part cinnamon schnapps
1 part orange juice
1 part vodka
Shake with ice and strain into a shot glass.

PENALTY SHOT

1 part crème de menthe
1 part coffee liqueur
1 part peppermint schnapps
Layer in a shot glass.

PEPPERITA

1 part tequila
1 part lemon juice
4 dashes of hot sauce
Pinch of salt

Rub the rim of a shot glass with lemon juice
and dip rim in salt. Shake the tequila and
the lemon juice with ice then strain into
the salt-rimmed glass. Add the hot sauce.

PEPPERMINT BANANA

1 part crème de banana
1 part peppermint schnapps

Shake with ice and strain into a shot glass.

PEPPERMINT BONBON

1 part peppermint schnapps
Dash of chocolate syrup

Layer in a shot glass.

PEPPERMINT PATTIE 1
1 part coffee liqueur
1 part peppermint schnapps
1 part half 'n half
Shake with ice and strain into a shot glass.

PEPPERMINT PATTIE 2
1 part 100-proof peppermint schnapps
Splash of chocolate syrup
Shake with ice and strain into a shot glass.

P.H.
1 part Southern Comfort®
1 part amaretto
1 part pineapple juice
Dash of lime juice
Layer in a shot glass.

PHOTON TORPEDO
1 part cinnamon schnapps
1 part vodka
Shake with ice and strain into a shot glass.

PIECE OF ASS, A
1 part amaretto
1 part Southern Comfort®
Splash of sour mix
Shake first two ingredients with ice
and strain into a shot glass.
Top with sour mix.

PIERCED BUTTERY NIPPLE
1 part butterscotch schnapps
1 part Irish cream
1 part Jägermeister®
Shake with ice and strain into a shot glass.

PIERCED NIPPLE
1 part sambuca
1 part Irish cream
Shake with ice and strain into a shot glass.

PIGSKIN SHOT
1 part vodka
1 part melon liqueur
1 part sour mix
Shake with ice and strain into a shot glass.

PINE SOL SHOOTER
1 part dark rum
1 part Frangelico®
Shake with ice and strain into a shot glass.

PINEAPPLE BOMB
1 part Southern Comfort®
1 part triple sec
1 part pineapple juice
Shake with ice and strain into a shot glass.

PINEAPPLE UPSIDE-DOWN CAKE
1 part Irish cream
1 part vodka
1 part butterscotch schnapps
1 part pineapple juice
Shake with ice and strain into a shot glass.

PINEBERRY

1 part cranberry vodka
1 part pineapple vodka
Lemon wedge

Shake with ice and strain into a shot glass.
Squeeze juice from the lemon wedge into
each glass.

PINK BELLY

1 part Jim Beam®
1 part amaretto
1 part sloe gin
1 part Irish cream
1 part lemon lime soda

Shake with ice and strain into a shot glass.*

Note: Because this recipe includes many ingredients,
it's easier to make in volume, about 6 shots.

PINK CADILLAC
1 part vodka
1 part cherry juice
1 part sour mix
1 part orange juice
Shake with ice and strain into a shot glass.

PINK FLOYD
1 part vodka
1 part peach schnapps
Splash of cranberry juice cocktail
Splash of grapefruit juice
Shake with ice and strain into a shot glass.

PINK GIN
1 part gin
Splash of cranberry juice cocktail
Shake with ice and strain into a shot glass.

PINK LEMONADE SHOOTER
1 part vodka
1 part sour mix
1 part cranberry juice cocktail
Shake with ice and strain into a shot glass.

PINK PETAL
1 part cinnamon schnapps
1 part Goldschläger®
Shake with ice and strain into a shot glass.

PINKY
1 part 100-proof peppermint schnapps
1 part Firewater®
Shake with ice and strain into a shot glass.

PIPELINE
1 part tequila
1 part vodka
Layer in a shot glass.

PISTOL SHOT
1 part triple sec
1 part apricot brandy
1 part cherry brandy
Shake with ice and strain into a shot glass.

PIT BULL ON CRACK
1 part Jägermeister®
1 part 100-proof peppermint schnapps
1 part tequila
Shake with ice and strain into a shot glass.

PIT BULL AND CRANK SHOOTER
1 part rum
1 part tequila
1 part Jägermeister®
1 part Seagrams 7® whiskey
1 part peppermint schnapps
Shake with ice and strain into a shot glass.

PLEAD THE FIFTH
1 part gin
1 part sambuca
1 part coffee liqueur
Shake with ice and strain into a shot glass.

PLEADING INSANITY
1 part tequila blanco
1 part vodka
1 part dark rum
Shake with ice and strain into a shot glass.

PLEASE JUST LEAVE ME HERE TO DIE!!!

1 part sambuca
1 part tequila gold
Splash of hot sauce
Layer in a shot glass.

P.M.F.

1 part 151-proof rum
1 part banana liqueur
1 part Irish cream
Layer in a shot glass.

POCO LOCO BOOM

1 part vodka
1 part Tia Maria®
1 part coconut cream
Shake with ice and strain into a shot glass.

POINT-BLANK
1 part brandy
1 part crème de banana
1 part apricot brandy
1 part cherry brandy
Shake with ice and strain into a shot glass.

POISON APPLE
1 part apple brandy
1 part vodka
Shake with ice and strain into a shot glass.

POISON IVY
1 part cinnamon schnapps
1 part coffee liqueur
Shake with ice and strain into a shot glass.

POISON MILK

1 part Jägermeister®
1 part Irish cream
Shake with ice and strain into a shot glass.

POLAR BEAR

1 part white crème de cacao
1 part peppermint schnapps
Shake with ice and strain into a shot glass.

POLISH POUNDER, THE

1 part coffee liqueur
1 part amaretto
1 part vodka
Layer in a shot glass.

POLLUTION
1 part Malibu Coconut Rum®
1 part melon liqueur
1 part pineapple juice
Shake with ice and strain into a shot glass.

PONDEROSA
1 part grain alcohol
1 part orange soda
Shake with ice and strain into a shot glass.

POOP CHUTE
2 parts black sambuca
1 part fruit punch
Shake with ice and strain into a shot glass.

PORTO COVO
1 part absinthe
1 part coconut liqueur
1 part banana liqueur
1 part vodka
Shake with ice and strain into a shot glass.

POWER DRILL
1 part vodka
1 part orange juice
Splash of beer
Layer in a shot glass.

POWER SHOT
1 part vodka
1 part pepper-flavored vodka
Pinch of wasabi
Shake with ice and strain into a shot glass.

PRAIRIE DOG
1 part 151-proof rum
3 dashes of hot sauce
Layer in a shot glass.

PRAIRIE FIRE
1 part tequila
5 dashes of hot sauce
Layer in a shot glass.

PRESTONE
1 part melon liqueur
2 parts citrus vodka
2 parts lemon lime soda
Shake with ice and strain into a shot glass.

PROTEIN SMOOTHIE
1 part scotch
1 part cream
1 part Clamato® juice
Shake with ice and strain into a shot glass.

PROZAC
1 part Crown Royal® bourbon
1 part melon liqueur
Splash of lemon lime soda
Shake with ice and strain into a shot glass.

P.S. I LOVE YOU
1 part Irish cream
1 part triple sec
Splash of crème de menthe
Shake with ice and strain into a shot glass.

PSYCHO TSUNAMI
1 part blue curaçao
1 part fresh lime juice
1 part tequila gold
Dash of hot sauce
Layer in a shot glass.

PUCKER SUCKER
1 part sour apple schnapps
1 part coffee liqueur
1 part orange juice
Shake with ice and strain into a shot glass.

PULL UP TO THE BUMPER
1 part Parfait Amour®
1 part peach schnapps
1 part gin
Shake with ice and strain into a shot glass.

PUMPKIN PIE

1 part Irish cream
1 part coffee liqueur
Dash of 151-proof rum
Splash of cinnamon schnapps
Shake with ice and strain into a shot glass.

PUPPY'S NOSE

1 part peppermint schnapps
1 part coffee liqueur
1 part Irish cream
Shake with ice and strain into a shot glass.

PURPLE ALASKAN THUNDER FUCK

1 part whiskey
1 part Southern Comfort®
1 part raspberry liqueur
1 part amaretto
Splash of pineapple juice
Splash of sour mix
Shake with ice and strain into a shot glass.*
*Note: Because this recipe includes many ingredients,
it's easier to make in volume, about 6 shots.

PURPLE ELASTIC THUNDER FUCK

1 part vodka
1 part Crown Royal® bourbon
1 part Southern Comfort®
1 part amaretto
1 part raspberry liqueur
Splash of pineapple juice
Splash of cranberry juice cocktail
Shake with ice and strain into shot glass.*

*Note: Because this recipe includes many ingredients,
it's easier to make in volume, about 6 shots.

PURPLE HAZE

1 part amaretto
1 part root beer schnapps
1 part milk
1 part grape soda
Shake with ice and strain into a shot glass.

PURPLE HOOTER

1 part raspberry liqueur
1 part lemon lime soda
1 part vodka
Shake with ice and strain into a shot glass.

PURPLE LEI

1 part raspberry liqueur
1 part coconut rum
1 part pineapple juice
Shake with ice and strain into a shot glass.

PURPLE NIPPLE

1 part Jägermeister®
1 part melon liqueur
1 part cranberry juice cocktail
Splash of orange juice
Shake with ice and strain into a shot glass.

PURPLE RAIN
1 part vodka
1 part blue curaçao
Splash of cranberry juice cocktail
Shake with ice and strain into a shot glass.

PURPLE VIPER
1 part sloe gin
1 part vodka
1 part raspberry liqueur
Shake with ice and strain into a shot glass.

PURPLE VW
2 parts blue curaçao
1 part grenadine
Shake with ice and strain into a shot glass.

PURPLE WIND

1 part raspberry liqueur
2 parts warm sake
Layer in a shot glass.

PURPLE-HELMETED WARRIOR

1 part gin
1 part Southern Comfort®
1 part peach schnapps
1 part blue curaçao
1 part lime juice
1 part grenadine
Splash of lemon lime soda
Shake with ice and strain into a shot glass.*

Note: Because this recipe contains many ingredients,
it's easier to make in volume, about 6 shots.

PUSSY JUICE

1 part Goldschläger®
1 part vodka
1 part vegetable juice
Shake with ice and strain into a shot glass.

PYRO

1 part vodka
1 part Firewater®
Splash of grain alcohol
Layer in a shot glass. Float the grain on top.
Light the grain with a lighter or match.
Extinguish by placing an empty shot glass
over the shot. Always extinguish the flame
before consuming.

QUICK CHECK
1 part peach schnapps
1 part triple sec
1 part cranberry juice cocktail
1 part orange juice
Shake with ice and strain into a shot glass.

R AND B (RYE AND BAILEYS)
1 part Baileys® Irish cream
1 part rye whiskey
Shake with ice and strain into a shot glass.

RABBIT PUNCH
1 part Campari®
1 part dark crème de cacao
1 part Irish cream
1 part coconut rum
Shake with ice and strain into a shot glass.

RAGING BULL

1 part coffee liqueur
1 part sambuca
1 part tequila
Layer in a shot glass.

RAGING INDIAN

1 part grain alcohol
1 part coffee liqueur
1 part orange juice
1 part mango nectar
Shake with ice and strain into a shot glass.

RAIDER

1 part Irish cream
1 part triple sec
1 part Cointreau®
Layer in a shot glass.

RAIJA

1 part coffee liqueur
1 part vanilla schnapps
1 part orange juice
1 part mango juice
Shake with ice and strain into a shot glass.

RAINBOW COCKTAIL
(BARTENDER'S CHALLENGE)

1 part blue curaçao
1 part green crème de menthe
1 part cognac
1 part maraschino liqueur
1 part blackberry liqueur
1 part crème de cassis
Layer in a shot glass.

Note: Because this recipe includes many ingredients,
it's easier to make in volume, about 6 shots.

RASPBERRY TOOTSIE ROLL POP

1 part amaretto
1 part raspberry liqueur
1 part vodka
1 part cola
1 part sweet and sour mix

Shake with ice and strain into a shot glass.*

*Note: Because this recipe includes many ingredients,
it's easier to make in volume, about 6 shots.

RASPBERRY BROWNIE

1 part coffee liqueur
1 part raspberry liqueur
Splash of cream

Layer in a shot glass.

RATTLESNAKE

1 part Irish cream
1 part coffee liqueur
1 part white crème de cacao
Layer in a shot glass.

RATTLESNAKE SHOOTER

1 part Irish cream
1 part Southern Comfort®
Layer in a shot glass.

RAZOR BLADE

1 part Jägermeister®
1 part 151-proof rum
Pour ingredients into glass neat
(do not chill).

READY, SET, GO

1 part crème de banana
1 part melon liqueur
1 part strawberry schnapps
Shake with ice and strain into a shot glass.

READY TO GO

1 part 151-proof rum
1 part triple sec
1 part grenadine
Shake with ice and strain into a shot glass.

REAL PISSER

1 part tequila
1 part Mountain Dew®
Layer in a shot glass.

REAL STRONG DIRTY ROTTEN SCOUNDREL, A
1 part cranberry-flavored vodka
Splash of melon liqueur
Shake with ice and strain into a shot glass.

REALITY TWIST
1 part amaretto
1 part blue curaçao
Layer in a shot glass.

REBEL JESTER
1 part kiwi liqueur
1 part cinnamon schnapps
Shake with ice and strain into a shot glass.

REBOOT

1 part green crème de menthe
1 part cachaça
1 part pepper-flavored vodka
Shake with ice and strain into a shot glass.

RED BARON

1 part Crown Royal® bourbon
1 part amaretto
Splash of cranberry juice cocktail
Shake with ice and strain into a shot glass.

RED BEARD

1 part spiced rum
1 part coconut rum
Splash of grenadine
Splash of lemon lime soda
Shake with ice and strain into a shot glass.

RED DEATH
1 part vodka
1 part Firewater®
1 part Yukon Jack®
1 part 151-proof rum
Shake with ice and strain into a shot glass.

RED DRAGON'S BREATH
1 part cinnamon schnapps
1 part whiskey
Shake with ice and strain into a shot glass.

RED HOT
1 part cinnamon schnapps
1 part tequila
Dash of hot sauce
Layer in a shot glass.

RED LOBSTER
1 part amaretto
1 part Southern Comfort®
Splash of cranberry juice cocktail
Shake with ice and strain into a shot glass.

RED MONSTER
1 part tequila
1 part orange juice
Shake with ice and strain into a shot glass.

RED ROYAL SHOT
1 part Crown Royal® bourbon
1 part amaretto
Shake with ice and strain into a shot glass.

RED SNAPPER
1 part Crown Royal® bourbon
1 part amaretto
Splash of cranberry juice cocktail
Shake with ice and strain into a shot glass.

RED SNAPPER SHOOTER
1 part whiskey
1 part amaretto
Shake with ice and strain into a shot glass.

RED SQUARE
1 part vodka
1 part sambuca
Shake with ice and strain into a shot glass.

REDBACK SHOOTER
1 part sambuca
1 part advocaat
Layer in a shot glass.

RED-EYED HELL
1 part vodka
1 part 151-proof rum
1 part spicy vegetable juice
1 part triple sec
Shake with ice and strain into a shot glass.

RED-EYED SHOOTER
1 part vodka
1 part crème de cassis
Shake with ice and strain into a shot glass.

RED-HEADED PRINCESS
1 part Jägermeister®
1 part peach schnapps
1 part cranberry juice cocktail
Shake with ice and strain into a shot glass.

RED-HEADED SLUT
1 part Jägermeister®
1 part peach schnapps
1 part cranberry juice cocktail
Shake with ice and strain into a shot glass.

RED-LINE
1 part tequila blanco
1 part sambuca
Splash of crème de cassis
Shake with ice and strain into a shot glass.

REDNECK MARINE

1 part Jägermeister®
1 part whiskey
1 part grain alcohol
Shake with ice and strain into a shot glass.

REPUBLICA DAS BANANAS

1 part tequila blanco
1 part rum
1 part crème de banana
Shake with ice and strain into a shot glass.

REVOLTO, EL

1 part peppermint schnapps
1 part Irish cream
1 part Cointreau®
Layer in a shot glass.

RHINO
1 part coffee liqueur
1 part Amarula Cream® liqueur
1 part Cointreau®
Layer in a shot glass.

RHYTHM AND BLUES
1 part whiskey
1 part blueberry schnapps
Shake with ice and strain into a shot glass.

RICH, CREAMY BUTTER
1 part vodka
1 teaspoon butter (melted)
Layer melted butter over chilled vodka in a
shot glass.

RICK
1 part sambuca
1 part orange juice
Shake with ice and strain into a shot glass.

RIDDLER, THE
1 part tequila
1 part triple sec
1 part melon liqueur
Layer in a shot glass.

ROADRUNNER PUNCH
1 part coconut rum
1 part blue curaçao
1 part peach schnapps
1 part fruit punch
Shake with ice and strain into a shot glass.

ROCK LOBSTER 1
1 part Irish cream
1 part amaretto
1 part white crème de cacao
Layer in a shot glass.

ROCK LOBSTER 2
1 part raspberry liqueur
1 part triple sec
1 part Crown Royal® bourbon
1 part cranberry juice cocktail
Shake with ice and strain into a shot glass.

ROCK STAR
1 part cinnamon schnapps
1 part sloe gin
1 part triple sec
1 part Jägermeister®
Shake with ice and strain into a shot glass.

ROCKET FUEL 1

1 part peppermint schnapps
1 part light rum
Shake with ice and strain into a shot glass.

ROCKET FUEL 2

1 part 151-proof rum
1 part vodka
1 part blue curaçao
Shake with ice and strain into a shot glass.

ROCKY MOUNTAIN

1 part Southern Comfort®
1 part amaretto
1 part lime juice
Shake with ice and strain into a shot glass.

ROCKY MOUNTAIN BUTTERFLY
1 part vodka
1 part Southern Comfort®
Dash of amaretto
Dash of sour mix
Shake with ice and strain into a shot glass.

ROLY-POLY
1 part triple sec
1 part peach schnapps
Shake with ice and strain into a shot glass.

ROMONA BANANA
1 part banana liqueur
1 part amaretto
1 part peppermint schnapps
Layer in a shot glass.

ROOSTER PISS
1 part whiskey
1 part cinnamon schnapps
Layer in a shot glass.

ROOSTER TAIL
1 part tequila
1 part orange juice
1 part tomato juice
Dash of salt
Layer in a shot glass. Lick your hand and
put a dash of salt on it, then lick the salt
and drink the shot.

ROOT BEER FLOAT
1 part root beer schnapps
1 part light cream
Layer in a shot glass.

ROOT BEER SHOOTER
1 part coffee liqueur
1 part Galliano®
1 part cola
Shake with ice and strain into a shot glass.

ROSSO DI SERA
1 part vodka
1 part strawberry schnapps
1 part triple sec
Shake with ice and strain into a shot glass.

ROT GUT
1 part cinnamon schnapps
1 part vodka
Shake with ice and strain into a shot glass.

ROYAL BITCH
1 part Frangelico®
1 part Crown Royal® bourbon
Shake with ice and strain into a shot glass.

ROYAL BUTT
1 part Crown Royal® bourbon
1 part butterscotch schnapps
Shake with ice and strain into a shot glass.

ROYAL DEAN
1 part blue curaçao
Splash of grenadine
Shake with ice and strain into a shot glass.

ROYAL FLUSH

1 part Crown Royal® bourbon
1 part peach schnapps
1 part cranberry juice cocktail
1 part orange juice
Shake with ice and strain into a shot glass.

ROYAL PEACH

1 part Crown Royal® bourbon
1 part peach schnapps
Shake with ice and strain into a shot glass.

ROYAL SCANDAL

1 part Crown Royal® bourbon
1 part Southern Comfort®
1 part amaretto
Splash of sweet and sour mix
Splash of pineapple juice
Shake with ice and strain into a shot glass.

RUBBER BISCUIT
1 part Crown Royal® bourbon
1 part butterscotch schnapps
Shake with ice and strain into a shot glass.

RUBY RED
1 part vodka
1 part cranberry juice cocktail
1 part sour mix
Shake with ice and strain into a shot glass.

RUGMUNCHER
1 part root beer schnapps
1 part Irish cream
Shake with ice and strain into a shot glass.

RUMKA

1 part vodka
1 part spiced rum
Shake with ice and strain into a shot glass.

RUNNY NOSE

1 part coffee liqueur
1 part Irish cream
1 part cherry liqueur
Layer in a shot glass.

RUSSIAN APPLE

1 part vodka
1 part cranberry juice cocktail
1 part pineapple juice
Shake with ice and strain into a shot glass.

RUSSIAN BALLET
1 part vodka
1 part crème de cassis
Shake with ice and strain into a shot glass.

RUSSIAN BLOODY MARY
1 part vodka
2 drops of hot sauce
Shake with ice and strain into a shot glass.

RUSSIAN CANDY
1 part vodka
1 part peach schnapps
Dash of grenadine
Shake with ice and strain into a shot glass.

RUSSIAN DEFECT
1 part vodka
1 part peppermint schnapps
Shake with ice and strain into a shot glass.

RUSSIAN QUAALUDE
1 part coffee liqueur
1 part vodka
1 part half 'n half
1 part Frangelico®
Shake with ice and strain into a shot glass.

RUSSIAN ROULETTE
1 shot vodka (warm)
Shot glasses of water
Fill one shot glass with warm vodka and all
additional shot glasses (one for each person)
with water. Mix up the glasses and hand
them out.

RUSSIAN SHAMROCK
1 part vodka
1 part crème de menthe
Shake with ice and strain into a shot glass.

RUSTY NAVEL
1 part tequila
1 part amaretto
Shake with ice and strain into a shot glass.

RUSTY SPIKE
1 part Drambuie®
1 part scotch
Layer in a shot glass.

SHIT
1 part sambuca
1 part Haagen Dazs® cream liqueur
1 part Irish Mist®
1 part tequila
Shake with ice and strain into a shot glass.

SABRA
1 part orange-flavored vodka
1 part chocolate liqueur
Shake with ice and strain into a shot glass.

SACRELICIOUS
1 part lemon lime–flavored rum
1 part melon liqueur
1 part lime juice
Shake with ice and strain into a shot glass.

SALHMAN
1 part amaretto
1 orange juice
2 parts tequila
1 part triple sec
Shake with ice and strain into a shot glass.

SAMBUCA SLIDE
1 part sambuca
1 part vodka
1 part light cream
Shake with ice and strain into a shot glass.

SAMBUCA SURPRISE

1 part white crème de cacao
1 part peppermint schnapps
1 part sambuca
Shake with ice and strain into a shot glass.

SAMMY SLAMMER

1 part Southern Comfort®
1 part vanilla schnapps
1 part peach schnapps
Shake with ice and strain into a shot glass.

SAMPLE

1 part grain alcohol
1 part lemon lime sports drink
Layer in a shot glass.

SAND BAG
1 part tequila
1 part Jägermeister®
Pinch of salt
Layer in a shot glass with a pinch of
salt on top.

SAND SLIDE
1 part vodka
1 part coffee liqueur
Shake with ice and strain into a shot glass.

SANDBLASTER
1 part cola
1 part light rum
1 part fresh lime juice
Shake with ice and strain into a shot glass.

SANDY BEACH
1 part Irish cream
1 part butterscotch schnapps
1 part amaretto
Splash of cream
Shake with ice and strain into a shot glass.

SANGRITA
1 part tequila
1 part Clamato® juice
2 drops of hot sauce
Dash of Worchestershire sauce
Shake with ice and strain into a shot glass.

SANTA CLAUS IS COMING
1 part 100-proof peppermint schnapps
1 part cinnamon schnapps
1 part melon liqueur
Layer in a shot glass and top with
whipped cream.

SARATOGA TRUNK
1 part tequila blanco
1 part Tia Maria®
1 part cinnamon schnapps
Shake with ice and strain into a shot glass.

SATAN'S MOUTHWASH
1 part whiskey
1 part sambuca
Layer in a shot glass.

SATAN'S REVENGE

1 part tequila
1 part whiskey
1 part Goldschläger®
Dash of hot sauce
Shake with ice and strain into a shot glass.

SCARLET O'HARA SHOOTER

1 part Southern Comfort®
1 part sweet and sour mix
1 part grenadine
Shake with ice and strain into a shot glass.

SCOOBY SNACK 1

1 part melon liqueur
1 part pineapple juice
1 part coconut rum
1 part cream
Shake with ice and strain into a shot glass.

SCOOBY SNACK 2
1 part coffee liqueur
1 part Irish cream
1 part 100-proof peppermint schnapps
1 part Jägermeister®
Shake with ice and strain into a shot glass.

SCORPION SHOOTER
1 part vodka
1 part blackberry liqueur
Shake with ice and strain into a shot glass.

SCORPION SUICIDE
1 part cherry brandy
1 part whiskey
1 part Pernod®
Shake with ice and strain into a shot glass.

SCREAMER

1 part gin
1 part rum
1 part tequila
1 part triple sec
Splash of vodka

Shake with ice and strain into a shot glass.

SCREAMING BLUE MESSIAH

1 part Goldschläger®
1 part blue curaçao

Shake with ice and strain into a shot glass.

SCREAMING COSMONAUT

1 part vodka
1 teaspoon powdered Tang®

Shake with ice and strain into a shot glass.

SCREAMING CRANAPPLE SHOOTER
1 part vodka
1 part Apfelkorn®
Shake with ice and strain into a shot glass.

SCREAMING GREEN MONSTER
1 part coconut rum
1 part melon liqueur
1 part 151-proof rum
1 part pineapple juice
1 part lemon lime soda
Shake with ice and strain into a shot glass.*
*Note: Because this recipe includes many ingredients,
it's easier to make in volume, about 6 shots.

SCREAMING LIZARD
1 part tequila
1 part Green Chartreuse®
Layer in a shot glass.

SCREAMING MOOSE
1 part Jägermeister®
1 part coffee liqueur
1 part Irish cream
Shake with ice and strain into a shot glass.

SCREAMING NAZI
1 part Jägermeister®
1 part 100-proof peppermint schnapps
Shake with ice and strain into a shot glass.

SCREAMING ORGASM SHOOTER
1 part vodka
1 part coffee liqueur
1 part Irish cream
Splash of amaretto
Shake with ice and strain into a shot glass.

SCREAMING YODA

1 part melon liqueur
1 part Jägermeister®
1 part orange juice
Shake with ice and strain into a shot glass.

SCREW 'N NAIL

1 part crème de banana
1 part cherry brandy
1 part chocolate mint liqueur
Shake with ice and strain into a shot glass.

SCURVY

1 part scotch
1 part coconut rum
1 part Irish cream
Layer in a shot glass.

SEA MONKEY

1 part Goldschläger®
1 part blue curaçao
Layer in a shot glass.

SECOND CHILDHOOD

1 part peppermint schnapps
1 part vodka
Shake with ice and strain into a shot glass.

SEDUCTION

1 part Frangelico®
1 part crème de banana
1 part Irish cream
Layer in a shot glass.

SEEING STARS

1 part peppermint schnapps
1 part coffee liqueur
1 part crème de banana
Shake with ice and strain into a shot glass.

SEÑOR TAZZ

1 part raspberry liqueur
1 part tequila
Shake with ice and strain into a shot glass.

SEX ON ACID

1 part Jägermeister®
1 part melon liqueur
1 part blackberry liqueur
1 part pineapple juice
1 part cranberry juice cocktail
Shake with ice and strain into a shot glass.*
*Note: Because this recipe contains many ingredients,
it's easier to make in volume, about 6 shots.

SEX ON THE BEACH
1 part vodka
1 part peach schnapps
1 part cranberry juice cocktail
1 part orange juice
Shake with ice and strain into a shot glass.

SEX ON THE LAKE
1 part crème de banana
1 part dark crème de cacao
1 part cream
Dash of light rum
Shake with ice and strain into a shot glass.

SEX AT MY HOUSE
1 part amaretto
1 part raspberry liqueur
1 part pineapple juice
Shake with ice and strain into a shot glass.

SEX IN THE PARKING LOT
1 part raspberry liqueur
1 part vodka
1 part sour apple schnapps
Shake with ice and strain into a shot glass.

SEX IN A VOLKSWAGEN
1 part grenadine
1 part sweetened lime juice
1 part white tequila
Splash of 151-proof rum
Shake with ice and strain into a shot glass.

SEX UNDER THE MOONLIGHT
1 part vodka
1 part coffee liqueur
1 part port
Splash of cream
Shake with ice and strain into a shot glass.

SEX UP AGAINST THE WALL SHOOTER

1 part currant-flavored vodka
1 part pineapple juice
1 part sweet and sour mix
Shake with ice and strain into a shot glass.

SEX WITH AN ALLIGATOR

1 part Jägermeister®
1 part melon liqueur
1 part raspberry liqueur
1 part pineapple juice
Shake with ice and strain into a shot glass.

SEX WITH A CHEERLEADER
1 part grenadine
1 part melon liqueur
1 part peppermint schnapps
1 part 151-proof rum
Layer in a shot glass. Top with
whipped cream.

SEXUAL STIMULATION
1 part rum
1 part green crème de menthe
1 part crème de banana
Shake with ice and strain into a shot glass.

SEXY ALLIGATOR

1 part coconut rum
1 part melon liqueur
1 part pineapple juice
1 part Jägermeister®
1 part raspberry liqueur

Shake with ice and strain into a shot glass.*

Note: Because this recipe includes many ingredients,
it's easier to make in volume, about 6 shots.

SHADE

1 part rum
1 part triple sec
1 part green crème de menthe
1 part sweet and sour mix

Shake with ice and strain into a shot glass.

SHAKE THAT ASS
1 part blue curaçao
1 part banana liqueur
1 part sour mix
1 part orange juice
Shake with ice and strain into a shot glass.

SHAMROCK SHOOTER
1 part crème de menthe
1 part white crème de cacao
1 part Irish cream
Layer in a shot glass.

SHAZAM SHOOTER
1 part sour apple schnapps
1 part raspberry liqueur
1 part cranberry juice cocktail
Shake with ice and strain into a shot glass.

SHIPWRECK SHOOTER
1 part light rum
1 part crème de banana
1 part sweet and sour mix
1 part strawberry schnapps
Shake with ice and strain into a shot glass.

SHIT ON GRASS
1 part melon liqueur
1 part coffee liqueur
Layer in a shot glass.

SHITTIN' BLUE
1 part vodka
1 part blueberry schnapps
1 part blue curaçao
Shake with ice and strain into a shot glass.

SHIVY JUICE
1 part 151-proof rum
1 part triple sec
1 part Jim Beam®
1 part grenadine
Shake with ice and strain into a shot glass.

SHOGUN SHOOTER
1 part citrus vodka
1 part melon liqueur
Shake with ice and strain into a shot glass.

SHOT IN THE BACK
1 part vodka
1 part cinnamon schnapps
Dash of wasabi
Shake with ice and strain into a shot glass.

SHOT OF RESPECT
1 part tequila
1 part 151-proof rum
Dash of hot sauce
Shake with ice and strain into a shot glass.

SHOTGUN
1 part Jim Beam®
1 part whiskey
1 part Wild Turkey®
Shake with ice and strain into a shot glass.

SHOT-O-HAPPINESS
1 part Goldschläger®
1 part raspberry schnapps
Splash of pineapple juice
Splash of sweet and sour mix
Splash of lemon lime soda
Shake with ice and strain into a shot glass.*
*Note: Because this recipe includes many ingredients,
it's easier to make in volume, about 6 shots.

SIBERIAN TOOLKIT
1 part vodka
1 part whiskey
Shake with ice and strain into a shot glass.

SICILIAN KISS
1 part amaretto
1 part Southern Comfort®
Shake with ice and strain into a shot glass.

SICILIAN SUNSET

1 part orange juice
1 part amaretto
1 part grenadine
1 part Southern Comfort®
Shake with ice and strain into a shot glass.
Place a few drops
of grenadine in the center for a sunset effect.

SILK PANTIES

1 part vodka
1 part peach schnapps
Shake with ice and strain into a shot glass.

SILLY SURFER
1 part blue curaçao
1 part peppermint schnapps
1 part Irish cream
Splash of 151-proof rum
Layer in a shot glass.

SILVER BULLET 1
1 part gin
1 part scotch
Lemon twist
Shake with ice and strain into a shot glass.
Garnish with a lemon twist.

SILVER BULLET 2
1 part Southern Comfort®
1 part whiskey
Shake with ice and strain into a shot glass.

SILVER BULLET 3
1 part ouzo
1 part 100-proof peppermint schnapps
Shake with ice and strain into a shot glass.

SILVER BULLET 4
1 part tequila
1 part crème de menthe
Shake with ice and strain into a shot glass.

SILVER DEVIL
1 part tequila
1 part peppermint schnapps
Shake with ice and strain into a shot glass.

SILVER SPIDER

1 part vodka
1 part rum
1 part triple sec
1 part white crème de cacao
Shake with ice and strain into a shot glass.

SILVER THREAD

1 part banana liqueur
1 part Irish cream
1 part peppermint schnapps
Layer in a shot glass.

SIMPLY BONKERS

1 part cream
1 part light rum
Shake with ice and strain into a shot glass.

SIMPSON BRONCO

1 part sambuca
1 part grenadine
1 part orange juice
Shake with ice and strain into a shot glass.

SINFUL APPLE

1 part vodka
1 part Apfelkorn®
Shake with ice and strain into a shot glass.

SIT ON MY FACE, MARY JANE

1 part Irish cream
1 part Frangelico®
1 part Crown Royal® bourbon
Shake with ice and strain into a shot glass.

SIT ON MY FACE, SAMMY

1 part Crown Royal® bourbon
1 part Frangelico®
1 part Irish cream
Shake with ice and strain into a shot glass.

SKID MARK

1 part coffee liqueur
1 part Jägermeister®
1 part 100-proof peppermint schnapps
Shake with ice and strain into a shot glass.

SKULL

1 part coffee liqueur
1 part Irish cream
1 part whiskey
Shake with ice and strain into a shot glass.

SLAM DUNK SHOOTER

1 part tequila gold
1 part lime cordial
1 part soda water
Shake with ice and strain into a shot glass.

SLAMMER

1 part tequila
1 part lemon lime soda
Pour ingredients into a glass neat (do not chill). Cover the top of the glass with the palm of your hand, slam the shot on the bar, and drink while it's fizzing.

SLANG

1 part gold rum
1 part vanilla schnapps
Shake with ice and strain into a shot glass.

SLAP SHOT
1 part Southern Comfort®
1 part peppermint schnapps
Shake with ice and strain into a shot glass.

SLICE OF APPLE PIE
1 part vodka
1 part apple juice
Shake with ice and strain into a shot glass.

SLICK AND SLEAZY
Splash of salsa
1 part vodka
Layer in a shot glass.

SLICKSTER

1 part Southern Comfort®
1 part peach schnapps
1 part lemon lime soda
Shake with ice and strain into a shot glass.

SLIPPERY CRICKET

1 part Maui Blue Hawaiian Schnapps®
1 part tropical schnapps
1 part vodka
Shake with ice and strain into a shot glass.

SLIPPERY NIPPLE

1 part Irish cream
1 part butterscotch schnapps
Shake with ice and strain into a shot glass.

SLIPPERY SADDLE
1 part vodka
1 part Licor 43®
1 part orange juice
Shake with ice and strain into a shot glass.

SLOE SLOP
1 part vodka
1 part sloe gin
1 part lemon lime soda
Shake with ice and strain into a shot glass.

SLOPE SURVIVAL POTION
1 part Wild Turkey®
1 part 100-proof peppermint schnapps
Shake with ice and strain into a shot glass.

SLOPPY BLOW JOB, A
1 part cream
1 part vodka
Shake with ice and strain into a shot glass.
Garnish with whipped cream.

SLUT JUICE
1 part vodka
1 part orange juice
1 part lemonade
Shake with ice and strain into a shot glass.

SMARTIE
1 part grape schnapps
1 part melon liqueur
Shake with ice and strain into a shot glass.

SMARTY

1 part amaretto
1 part Southern Comfort®
1 part blackberry brandy
1 part sour mix
Shake with ice and strain into a shot glass.

SMASHING PUMPKIN

1 part coffee liqueur
1 part Irish cream
1 part Goldschläger®
Shake with ice and strain into a shot glass.

SMEGMA DELIGHT

1 part vodka
2 dashes of Parmesan cheese
Layer in a shot glass.

SMELLY SHOES
1 part amaretto
1 part Blavod® black vodka
Layer in a shot glass.

SMILES
1 part peppermint schnapps
1 part amaretto
1 part whiskey
Shake with ice and strain into a shot glass.

SMOKE CURTAIN
1 part vodka
1 part gold rum
1 part triple sec
Splash of lime juice
Shake with ice and strain into a shot glass.

SMOOTH AND SWEET
1 part amaretto
1 part blackberry liqueur
1 part pineapple juice
Shake with ice and strain into a shot glass.

SMOOTH DOG
1 part amaretto
1 part lemon lime soda
Pour ingredients into a glass neat
(do not chill).

SMOOTH NIPPLE
1 part coffee liqueur
1 part butterscotch schnapps
Shake with ice and strain into a shot glass.

SMOOTHIE

1 part Crown Royal® bourbon
1 part amaretto
Splash of triple sec
Splash of sour mix
Splash of lemon lime soda

Shake with ice and strain into a shot glass.*

*Note: Because this recipe includes many ingredients,
it's easier to make in volume, about 6 shots.

SMURF FART

1 part blue curaçao
1 part blueberry schnapps
Splash of cream

Shake with ice and strain into a shot glass.

SMURF ON THE RAG
1 part peach schnapps
1 part blue curaçao
Splash of grenadine
Shake peach schnapps and blue curaçao with ice and strain into a shot glass. Top with whipped cream and add a few drops of grenadine on top.

SMURF PISS
1 part blue curaçao
2 parts ginger ale
Shake with ice and strain into a shot glass.

SNAKE BITE
1 part Yukon Jack®
Dash of lime juice
Shake with ice and strain into a shot glass.

SNAPPLE SHOOTER
1 part cranberry juice cocktail
1 part orange juice
1 part vodka
1 part triple sec
Shake with ice and strain into a shot glass.

SNAPSHOT
1 part peppermint schnapps
1 part Irish cream
Layer in a shot glass.

SNATCH, CRACKLE, AND POP
1 part grenadine
1 part vodka
3 dashes of Pop Rocks® candy
Shake with ice and strain into a shot glass.

SNEAKERS
1 part amaretto
1 part pineapple juice
1 part vodka
Shake with ice and strain into a shot glass.

SNEEKER
1 part raspberry liqueur
1 part coconut rum
1 part 151-proof rum
1 part melon liqueur
1 part cranberry juice cocktail
1 part lemon lime soda
Shake with ice and strain into a shot glass.*

*Note: Because this recipe includes many ingredients,
it's easier to make in volume, about 6 shots.

SNICKERS

1 part dark crème de cacao
1 part Frangelico®
Shake with ice and strain into a shot glass.

SNOTTY TODDY

1 part melon liqueur
1 part 151-proof rum
1 part orange juice
Shake with ice and strain into a shot glass.

SNOW CAP

1 part Irish cream
1 part tequila
Layer in a shot glass.

SNOW DROP SHOOTER
1 part cream
1 part white crème de cacao
1 part vodka
1 part triple sec
Shake with ice and strain into a shot glass.

SNOW MELTER
1 part sambuca
1 part white crème de cacao
1 part rum
Shake with ice and strain into a shot glass.

SNOWBALL
1 part whiskey
1 part 100-proof peppermint schnapps
Shake with ice and strain into a shot glass.

SNOWBALL'S CHANCE IN HELL
1 part cinnamon schnapps
1 part 100-proof peppermint schnapps
Shake with ice and strain into a shot glass.

SNOWSHOE
1 part vodka
1 part peppermint schnapps
Shake with ice and strain into a shot glass.

SNOWSHOE (FRENCH)
1 part peppermint schnapps
1 part brandy
Shake with ice and strain into a shot glass.

SNOWSHOE (TENNESSEE)
1 part peppermint schnapps
1 part bourbon
Shake with ice and strain into a shot glass.

SNOWSNAKE JUICE
1 part Crown Royal® bourbon
1 part peppermint schnapps
Shake with ice and strain into a shot glass.

SO CO SLAMMER
1 part cola
1 part Southern Comfort®
Pour ingredients into a glass neat
(do not chill).

SOFT BEDROCK, A
1 part sambuca
1 part coffee liqueur
Splash of milk
Shake first two with ice and strain into a
shot glass. Top with a splash of milk.

SOLAR FLARE
1 part vodka
1 part triple sec
Shake with ice and strain into a shot glass.

SON OF A BEACH SHOT
1 part vodka
1 part lemon lime soda
1 part blue curaçao
Shake with ice and strain into a shot glass.

SONGBIRD
1 part tequila silver
1 part vodka
1 part crème de banana
Shake with ice and strain into a shot glass.

SOOTHER

1 part amaretto
1 part melon liqueur
1 part vodka
1 part sour mix
Shake with ice and strain into a shot glass.

SOUL TAKER

1 part vodka
1 part tequila
1 part amaretto
Shake with ice and strain into a shot glass.

SOUR GRAPES

1 part sour mix
1 part vodka
1 part raspberry liqueur
Shake with ice and strain into a shot glass.

SOUR GRAPES SHOOTER
1 part vodka
1 part sweet and sour mix
Shake with ice and strain into a shot glass.

SOUR LEMON
1 part sweet and sour mix
1 part citrus vodka
1 part lime cordial
Shake with ice and strain into a shot glass.

SOUTHERN BELLE
1 part apricot brandy
1 part amaretto
1 part Southern Comfort®
Layer in a shot glass.

SOUTHERN BITCH

1 part amaretto
1 part peach schnapps
1 part pineapple juice
1 part orange juice
1 part Southern Comfort®
Shake with ice and strain into a shot glass.

SOUTHERN BLUES

1 part Southern Comfort®
1 part blueberry schnapps
Shake with ice and strain into a shot glass.

SOUTHERN BONDAGE
1 part Southern Comfort®
1 part amaretto
1 part peach schnapps
1 part triple sec
Splash of cranberry juice cocktail
Splash of sour mix
Shake with ice and strain into a shot glass.*

*Note: Because this recipe includes many ingredients,
it's easier to make in volume, about 6 shots.

SOUTHERN BRAIN DAMAGE
2 parts Southern Comfort®
1 part coffee liqueur
3 drops of grenadine
Shake with ice and strain into a shot glass.

SOUTHERN CHASE
1 part Galliano®
1 part Southern Comfort®
1 part Jim Beam®
Shake with ice and strain into a shot glass.

SOUTHERN FRUITY PASSION
1 part Southern Comfort®
1 part triple sec
1 part grenadine
Shake with ice and strain into a shot glass.

SOUTHERN JOE
1 part Southern Comfort®
1 part whiskey
Shake with ice and strain into a shot glass.

SOUTHERN PALM
1 part Drambuie®
1 part peppermint schnapps
Shake with ice and strain into a shot glass.

SOUTHERN PEACH
1 part peach schnapps
1 part Southern Comfort®
Shake with ice and strain into a shot glass.

SOUTHERN PINK FLAMINGO
1 part Southern Comfort®
1 part coconut rum
Splash of pineapple juice
Dash of grenadine
Dash of lemon juice
Shake with ice and strain into a shot glass.

SOUTHERN SEX ON THE BEACH SHOOTER (NY)

1 part peach schnapps
1 part pineapple juice
1 part Southern Comfort®
Shake with ice and strain into a shot glass.

SOUTHERN SMILE

1 part Southern Comfort®
1 part amaretto
Splash of cranberry juice cocktail
Shake with ice and strain into a shot glass.

SPACE ODYSSEY

1 part 151-proof rum
1 part coconut rum
1 part pineapple juice
Shake with ice and strain into a shot glass.

SPANISH MOSS (SHOOTER)
1 part coffee liqueur
1 part green crème de menthe
1 part tequila blanco
Shake with ice and strain into a shot glass.

SPARATO MILANO
1 part sambuca
1 part amaretto
1 part cherry brandy
Shake with ice and strain into a shot glass.

SPARK PLUG
1 part 151-proof rum
1 part 100-proof peppermint schnapps
Pour ingredients into a glass neat
(do not chill).

SPERM SHOT

1 part crème de banana
1 part cream
Shake with ice and strain into a shot glass.

SPERM WHALE

1 part cream
1 part rye whiskey
1 part Southern Comfort®
Shake with ice and strain into a shot glass.

SPICE CAKE

1 part Irish cream
1 part amaretto
1 part cinnamon schnapps
Shake with ice and strain into a shot glass.

SPICED APPLE
1 part apple brandy
1 part Goldschläger®
1 part spiced rum
Shake with ice and strain into a shot glass.

SPICED JOLLY ROGER
1 part cinnamon schnapps
1 part spiced rum
Shake with ice and strain into a shot glass.

SPICY APPLE
1 part cinnamon schnapps
1 part apple liqueur
Shake with ice and strain into a shot glass.

SPICY BUTTERY NIPPLE
1 part cinnamon schnapps
1 part butterscotch schnapps
1 part Irish cream
Shake with ice and strain into a shot glass.

SPIRITWALKER
1 part Jägermeister®
1 part 100-proof peppermint schnapps
1 part 151-proof rum
1 part Firewater®
Shake with ice and strain into a shot glass.

SPITFIRE
1 part whiskey
1 part rum
1 part vodka
Shake with ice and strain into a shot glass.

SPOT SHOOTER
1 part vodka
1 part coffee liqueur
Shake with ice and strain into a shot glass.

SPY CATCHER
1 part whiskey
1 part sambuca
Shake with ice and strain into a shot glass.

SQUIRREL'S FANTASY
1 part amaretto
1 part Frangelico®
1 part soda water
Shake with ice and strain into a shot glass.

SQUISHED SMURF

1 part peach schnapps
1 part Irish cream
1 part blue curaçao
Dash of grenadine
Shake with ice and strain into a shot glass.

SQUISHY

1 part raspberry liqueur
1 part amaretto
1 part vodka
Shake with ice and strain into a shot glass.

SR-71

1 part amaretto
1 part Irish cream
Shake with ice and strain into a shot glass.

STAINED BLUE DRESS
1 part vodka
1 part blue curaçao
2 drops of Irish cream
Layer in a shot glass.

STARS AND STRIPES
1 part blue curaçao
1 part heavy cream
1 part grenadine
Layer in a shot glass.

START ME UP
3 parts vodka
1 part tequila
1 part currant-flavored vodka
1 part dark rum
Shake with ice and strain into a shot glass.

STEAMBOAT

1 part vodka
1 part coffee liqueur
1 part whipped cream
Shake with ice and strain into a shot glass.

STEVIE RAY VAUGHN

1 part Irish cream
1 part Southern Comfort®
1 part triple sec
1 part sweet and sour mix
1 part orange juice
Shake with ice and strain into a shot glass.

STEVIE WONDER

1 part coffee liqueur
1 part dark crème de cacao
1 part amaretto
1 part Galliano®
Shake with ice and strain into a shot glass.

STIFF DICK

1 part butterscotch schnapps
1 part Irish cream
Shake with ice and strain into a shot glass.

STILETTO

1 part coffee liqueur
1 part peppermint schnapps
1 part tequila
Layer in a shot glass.

STINGER SHOOTER
1 part brandy
1 part peppermint schnapps
Layer in a shot glass.

STINGRAY
1 part vodka
1 part peppermint schnapps
Layer in a shot glass.

STINKY WEASEL
1 part tequila
1 part 151-proof rum
1 part lemon juice
2 dashes of sugar
Shake with ice and strain into a shot glass.

STOP AND GO
1 part currant-flavored vodka
1 part melon liqueur
1 part triple sec
Shake with ice and strain into a shot glass.

STOP-LIGHT
3 parts vodka
1 part melon liqueur
1 part orange juice
1 part cranberry juice cocktail
Shake with ice and strain into a shot glass.

STORM
1 part light rum
1 part blue curaçao
1 part Irish cream
Layer in a shot glass.

STORM CLOUD

1 part amaretto
Splash of 151-proof rum
1 part Irish cream
Layer in a shot glass.

STORM WARNING

1 part white crème de cacao
1 part Irish cream
1 part cherry liqueur
Layer in a shot glass.

STORMY

1 part black sambuca
1 part cream
Layer in a shot glass.

STRANDED IN TIJUANA
1 part sloe gin
1 part tequila gold
1 part 151-proof rum
Shake with ice and strain into a shot glass.

STRAWBERRY BLISS BOMB
1 part white crème de cacao
1 part strawberry schnapps
1 part coconut liqueur
Shake with ice and strain into a shot glass.

STRAWBERRY DROPPER
1 part amaretto
1 part peach schnapps
Splash of strawberry schnapps
Shake with ice and strain into a shot glass.

STRAWBERRY KISS
1 part coffee liqueur
1 part strawberry liqueur
1 part Irish cream
Layer in a shot glass.

STRAWBERRY LIPS
1 part cream
1 part coconut liqueur
1 part strawberry schnapps
Shake with ice and strain into a shot glass.

STREETCAR
1 part dark crème de cacao
1 part Irish cream
1 part apricot brandy
Layer in a shot glass.

STROKE

1 part banana liqueur
1 part Irish cream
3 drops of grenadine
Layer in a shot glass.

STUBBORN ITALIAN

1 part sambuca
Splash of Galliano®
Shake with ice and strain into a shot glass.

SUBLIME

1 part amaretto
1 part banana liqueur
1 part white crème de cacao
Layer in a shot glass.

SUICIDE
1 part vodka
2 parts lime cordial
2 parts club soda
Layer in a shot glass.

SUICIDE STOP-LIGHT
1 part melon liqueur
1 part vodka
1 part Aftershock® cinnamon schnapps
Splash of orange juice
Layer in a shot glass.

SUITABLY FRANK
1 part vodka
1 part cherry brandy
1 part Licor 43®
Layer in a shot glass.

SUMMER FLING
1 part blue curaçao
1 part Irish cream
Layer in a shot glass.

SUN AND SURF
1 part coffee liqueur
1 part triple sec
1 part tequila
Layer in a shot glass.

SUNNY DELIGHT, A
3 parts lemon-flavored vodka
1 part triple sec
1 part club soda
Shake with ice and strain into a shot glass.

SUNNY MEXICO
1 part Galliano®
1 part tequila
Layer in a shot glass.

SUNSET (NIGHT CLUB)
1 part watermelon schnapps
1 part coconut rum
1 part pineapple juice
Splash of grenadine
Shake with ice and strain into a shot glass.

SUNSET SHOOTER
1 part vodka
1 part grenadine
1 part lemon lime soda
1 part orange juice
Shake with ice and strain into a shot glass.

SUPER SCREW

1 part vodka
1 part soda water
1 part orange juice
Pour ingredients into a glass neat
(do not chill).

SUPERMODEL

1 part lemon lime–flavored rum
1 part melon liqueur
1 part blue curaçao
Shake with ice and strain into a shot glass.

SURFER ON ACID

1 part Jägermeister®
1 part coconut rum
1 part pineapple juice
Shake with ice and strain into a shot glass.

SWAMP THING
1 part coffee liqueur
1 part Irish cream
1 part crème de menthe
Shake with ice and strain into a shot glass.

SWAMP WATER
1 part orange juice
1 part pineapple juice
1 part Southern Comfort®
Shake with ice and strain into a shot glass.

SWEAT SOCK
1 part squeezing from a bar rag
Mop up any spills on the bar with a rag and
squeeze into a shot glass.

SWEDISH TRICOLOR
1 part banana liqueur
1 part blue curaçao
1 part vodka
Layer in a shot glass.

SWEDISH QUAALUDE
1 part vodka
1 part Frangelico®
Shake with ice and strain into a shot glass.

SWEET PEACH
1 part peach schnapps
1 part amaretto
Splash of orange juice
Shake with ice and strain into a shot glass.

SWEET PICKLE
1 part vodka
1 part 100-proof peppermint schnapps
1 part melon liqueur
Shake with ice and strain into a shot glass.

SWEET TART
1 part raspberry liqueur
1 part sour mix
1 part Southern Comfort®
Shake with ice and strain into a shot glass.

SWEET TART SHOOTERS
1 part amaretto
1 part raspberry liqueur
1 part sweet and sour mix
Shake with ice and strain into a shot glass.

SWEET TITS
1 part strawberry liqueur
1 part apricot brandy
Splash of pineapple juice
Shake with ice and strain into a shot glass.

SWELL SEX
1 part splash cream
1 part melon liqueur
Splash of pineapple juice
1 part coconut rum
1 part vodka
Shake with ice and strain into a shot glass.*

*Note: Because this recipe includes many ingredients,
it's easier to make in volume, about 6 shots.

SWIFT KICK IN THE BALLS
1 part rum
1 part vodka
1 part lemon juice
Shake with ice and strain into a shot glass.

SWISS HIKER
1 part amaretto
1 part crème de banana
1 part Irish cream
Layer in a shot glass.

SWISS AND WHOOSH
1 part coffee liqueur
1 part Frangelico®
1 part Irish cream
Layer in a shot glass.

TNT

1 part tequila
1 part tonic water
Pour ingredients into a glass neat
(do not chill).

T-52

1 part coffee liqueur
1 part Tequila Rose®
1 part triple sec
Layer in a shot glass.

TABLAZO
1 part ginger ale
1 part vodka
Pour ingredients into a glass neat
(do not chill).

TAINTED HEART
1 part cinnamon schnapps
1 part chocolate liqueur
Pour ingredients into a glass neat
(do not chill).

TAKE ME AWAY
1 part amaretto
1 part Irish cream
1 part peach brandy
Pour ingredients into a glass neat
(do not chill).

TAMPON IN THE TOILET

1 part peach schnapps
1 pimento from a large olive
Layer in a shot glass.

TART KART

1 part Goldschläger®
1 part banana liqueur
Shake with ice and strain into a shot glass.

TASTY ORGASM

1 part peppermint schnapps
1 part Irish cream
Shake with ice and strain into a shot glass.

T-BONE

1 part 151-proof rum
Splash A1® steak sauce
Layer in a shot glass.

TEDDY BEAR

1 part root beer schnapps
1 part vodka
Layer in a shot glass.

TEEN WOLF

1 part advocaat
1 part cherry liqueur
Shake with ice and strain into a shot glass.

TEQUILA BODY SLAMMER

Pinch of salt
1 part tequila
1 part lemon
Put salt on some part of somebody else's
body. Hold the shot glass in your left hand
and the lemon in the right. Lick the salt,
slam the tequila, and then suck lemon.

TEQUILA COMFORT
1 part tequila
1 part Southern Comfort®
Shake with ice and strain into a shot glass.

TEQUILA MOCKINGBIRD SHOOTER
1 part amaretto
1 part tequila
Layer in a shot glass.

TEQUILA ROSE
1 part tequila
1 triple sec
1 part cherry juice
1 part sweet and sour mix
Shake with ice and strain into a shot glass.

TEQUILA SLAMMER
1 part tequila
1 part lemon lime soda
Pour ingredients into a glass neat (do not chill). Cover the top of the glass with the palm of your hand, slam the shot on the bar, and drink while it's fizzing.

TERMINATOR
1 part Jägermeister®
1 part Southern Comfort®
Shake with ice and strain into a shot glass.

TEST TUBE BABY
1 part peach schnapps
1 part Irish cream
Dash of grenadine
Shake with ice and strain into a shot glass.

TETANUS SHOT

1 part Irish cream
1 part cherry brandy
1 part fruit schnapps
Shake with ice and strain into a shot glass.

TEXAS CHAINSAW MASSACRE

1 part strawberry liqueur
1 part vodka
Layer in a shot glass.

TEXAS MUD SLIDE, THE

1 part Crown Royal® bourbon
1 part coffee liqueur
1 part Irish cream
Layer in a shot glass.

TEXAS ROADKILL

1 part Wild Turkey®
1 part vodka
1 part gin
1 part 151-proof rum
Splash of hot sauce
Shake with ice and strain into a shot glass.

TEXAS SWEAT

1 part grain alcohol
Dash of grenadine
1 part vodka
1 part rum
1 part gin
1 part tequila
Shake with ice and strain into a shot glass.*

*Note: Because this recipe includes many ingredients,
it's easier to make in volume, about 6 shots.

TGV

1 part tequila
1 part gin
1 part vodka
Shake with ice and strain into a shot glass.

THORAZINE

1 part Jägermeister®
1 part 100-proof peppermint schnapps
1 part 151-proof rum
Layer in a shot glass. Float the 151-proof rum on top. Light the rum with a lighter or match. Extinguish by placing an empty shot glass over the shot. Always extinguish the flame before consuming.

THORNY ROSE
1 part Tequila Rose®
1 part peppermint schnapps
1 part coffee liqueur
Layer in a shot glass.

THREE SHEETS TO THE WIND
1 part Jägermeister®
1 part 100-proof peppermint schnapps
1 part tequila
Shake with ice and strain into a shot glass.

THREE WISE MEN (ORIGINAL)
1 part whiskey
1 part Jim Beam®
1 part tequila
Pour ingredients into a glass neat
(do not chill).

THREE WISE MEN 2
1 part Jägermeister®
1 part Goldschläger®
1 part Rumplemintz®
Shake with ice and strain into a shot glass.

THREE WISE MEN (ON A FARM)
1 part whiskey
1 part Jim Beam®
1 part Yukon Jack®
1 part Wild Turkey®
Pour ingredients into a glass neat
(do not chill).

THREE WISE MEN (VODKA)
1 part Jägermeister®
1 part vodka
1 part 100-proof peppermint schnapps
Pour ingredients into a glass neat
(do not chill).

THREE'S COMPANY
1 part Courvoisier®
1 part triple sec
1 part coffee liqueur
Layer in a shot glass.

THUG PASSION
1 part Alizé®
1 part vodka
Layer in a shot glass.

THUMBS UP

1 part crème de banana
1 part cherry brandy
1 part mango schnapps
Shake with ice and strain into a shot glass.

THUNDER AND LIGHTNING 1

1 part blackberry liqueur
1 part 151-proof rum
Shake with ice and strain into a shot glass.

THUNDER AND LIGHTNING 2

1 part peppermint schnapps
1 part 151-proof rum
Shake with ice and strain into a shot glass.

THUNDER CLOUD
1 part amaretto
1 part Irish Mist®
1 part 151-proof rum
Shake with ice and strain into a shot glass.

TIC TAC SHOOTER
1 part peppermint schnapps
1 part ouzo
Shake with ice and strain into a shot glass.

TIGER TAIL
1 part coffee liqueur
1 part triple sec
1 part peppermint schnapps
Shake with ice and strain into a shot glass.

T.K.O.
1 part sambuca
1 part coffee liqueur
1 part tequila
Shake with ice and strain into a shot glass.

TO THE MOON
1 part coffee liqueur
1 part amaretto
1 part Irish cream
1 part 151-proof rum
Shake with ice and strain into a shot glass.

TOASTED ALMOND (SHOOTER)
1 part amaretto
1 part cream
Shake with ice and strain into a shot glass.

TOE TAG
1 part Wild Turkey®
1 part whiskey
Shake with ice and strain into a shot glass.

TOFFEE APPLE
1 part vodka
1 part butterscotch schnapps
1 part sour apple schnapps
Shake with ice and strain into a shot glass.

TOOLKIT
1 part white crème de cacao
1 part Irish cream
1 part amaretto
1 part coffee liqueur
Shake with ice and strain into a shot glass.

TOOTSIE ROLL
1 part coffee liqueur
1 part orange juice
Shake with ice and strain into a shot glass.

TOOTSIE SHOT
1 part orange juice
1 part Jägermeister®
Shake with ice and strain into a shot glass.

TOP BANANA SHOOTER
1 part white crème de cacao
1 part vodka
1 part coffee liqueur
1 part crème de banana
Shake with ice and strain into a shot glass.

TOP DECK
1 part white crème de cacao
1 part chocolate syrup
Splash of cream
Layer in a shot glass.

TORO BRAVO, EL
1 part coffee liqueur
1 part tequila
Shake with ice and strain into a shot glass.

TORQUE WRENCH
1 part champagne
1 part orange juice
1 part melon liqueur
Layer in a shot glass.

TOSSED SALAD
1 part coffee liqueur
1 part Jägermeister®
Layer in a shot glass.

TOXIC JELLY BEAN
2 parts Jägermeister®
1 part ouzo
Splash of blackberry brandy
Layer in a shot glass.

TOXIC REFUSE
1 part vodka
1 part triple sec
1 part melon liqueur
Splash of lime juice
Shake with ice and strain into a shot glass.

TRAP DOOR
1 part amaretto
1 part rum cream liqueur
Layer in a shot glass.

TRIAL OF THE CENTURY
1 part Jägermeister®
1 part Goldschläger®
1 part grenadine
Layer in a shot glass.

TROPIC SLAMMER
1 part spiced rum
1 part coconut cream
1 part pineapple juice
Shake with ice and strain into a shot glass.

TROPICAL HOOTER
1 part raspberry liqueur
1 part lemon lime soda
1 part citrus vodka
1 part watermelon schnapps
Shake with ice and strain into a shot glass.

TROPICAL PASSION
1 part peach schnapps
1 part rum
1 part sloe gin
1 part triple sec
Splash of orange juice
Shake with ice and strain into a shot glass.*
*Note: Because this recipe includes many ingredients,
it's easier to make in volume, about 6 shots.

TURKEY SHOOT

1 part Wild Turkey 101®
1 part anisette
Shake with ice and strain into a shot glass.

TURKEYBALL

1 part Wild Turkey®
1 part amaretto
Splash of pineapple juice
Shake with ice and strain into a shot glass.

TWISTER SHOOTER 1

1 part vodka
1 part cherry brandy
1 part ouzo
Layer in a shot glass.

TWISTER SHOOTER 2

1 part Southern Comfort®
1 part tequila
1 part vodka
Layer in a shot glass.

U-2
1 part peppermint schnapps
1 part melon liqueur
Shake with ice and strain into a shot glass.

UARAPITO
1 part dark rum
1 part grenadine
1 part apple juice
Shake with ice and strain into a shot glass.

UNABOMBER
1 part gin
1 part vodka
1 part triple sec
1 part lime juice
Shake with ice and strain into a shot glass.

UNDER WATER
1 part blue curaçao
1 part Irish cream
1 part peach schnapps
Shake with ice and strain into a shot glass.

UNDERTAKER
1 part Jägermeister®
1 part Cointreau®
1 part 151-proof rum
Layer in a shot glass.

UNHOLY WATER

1 part gin
1 part grain alcohol
1 part spiced rum
1 part tequila
1 part vodka

Shake with ice and strain into a shot glass.*

Note: Because this recipe includes many ingredients,
it's easier to make in volume, about 6 shots.

UNLEADED

1 part dark rum
1 part tequila gold

Shake with ice and strain into a shot glass.

UPCHUCK

1 part 151-proof rum
1 part tequila
1 part Jägermeister®

Shake with ice and strain into a shot glass.

UPSIDE DOWN APPLE PIE SHOT
1 part apple juice
Dash of cinnamon
Squirt of whipped cream
1 part vodka
Shake with ice and strain into a shot glass.

UPSTARTER
1 part vodka
1 part peach schnapps
Shake with ice and strain into a shot glass.

URBAN COWBOY
1 part triple sec
1 part whiskey
1 part Southern Comfort®
Shake with ice and strain into a shot glass.

URINE SAMPLE

1 part Galliano®
1 part melon liqueur
1 part vodka
Shake with ice and strain into a shot glass.

UZI SHOOTER

1 part vermouth
1 part pastis
1 part sugar
Shake with ice and strain into a shot glass.

V-2 SCHNIEDER

1 part coffee liqueur
1 part Irish cream
1 part Frangelico®
Layer in a shot glass.

VAMPIRE JUICE

1 part coconut rum
1 part blue curaçao
1 part lemon lime–flavored rum
Splash of orange juice
Shake with ice and strain into a shot glass.

VANILLA ICE CREAM
1 part cream
1 part spiced rum
Dash of vanilla extract
Shake with ice and strain into a shot glass.

VANILLA KISS
1 part chocolate liqueur
1 part vanilla schnapps
Splash of cream
Shake with ice and strain into a shot glass.

VARICOSE VEINS
1 part Irish cream
1 part crème de menthe
Shake with ice and strain into a shot glass.

VENETIAN BLINDER
1 part dark crème de cacao
1 part 151-proof rum
Shake with ice and strain into a shot glass.

VIBRATOR
2 parts Southern Comfort®
1 part Irish cream
Layer in a shot glass.

VIKING FUNERAL
1 part 100-proof peppermint schnapps
1 part Jägermeister®
1 part Goldschläger®
Shake with ice and strain into a shot glass.

VILLA MASSA MOTHER PUCKER

1 part Villa Massa Liquore di Limoni®
1 part vodka
Shake with ice and strain into a shot glass.

VILLAGE

1 part vodka
1 part passion fruit liqueur
1 part pineapple juice
Shake with ice and strain into a shot glass.

VINE CLIMBER

1 part vodka
1 part melon liqueur
1 part sweet and sour mix
Shake with ice and strain into a shot glass.

VIPER

1 part vodka
1 part amaretto
1 part Malibu Coconut Rum®
1 part Midori®
1 part pineapple juice

Shake with ice and strain into a shot glass.*

*Note: Because this recipe includes many ingredients,
it's easier to make in volume, about 6 shots.

VIRULENT DEATH

1 part blue curaçao
1 part Yukon Jack®
1 part Galliano®

Shake with ice and strain into a shot glass.

VOCODER

1 part anisette
1 part mirabelle liqueur
1 part aquavit
1 part cinnamon schnapps
Shake with ice and strain into a shot glass.

VOLVO

1 part Cointreau®
1 part triple sec
1 part vodka
1 part cognac
1 part apricot brandy
Shake with ice and strain into a shot glass.*

*Note: Because this recipe includes many ingredients,
it's easier to make in volume, about 6 shots.

VOODOO 1
1 part black sambuca
1 part half 'n half
Shake with ice and strain into a shot glass.

VOODOO 2
1 part peppermint schnapps
1 part vodka
Shake with ice and strain into a shot glass.

VULCAN DEATH GRIP
1 part Goldschläger®
1 part rum
Shake with ice and strain into a shot glass.

VULCAN DEATH PROBE
1 part ouzo
1 part grain alcohol
Shake with ice and strain into a shot glass.

VULCAN MIND MELD
1 part ouzo
1 part 151-proof rum
Shake with ice and strain into a shot glass.

VULCAN MIND PROBE
1 part ouzo
1 part rum
Shake with ice and strain into a shot glass.

WALK ME DOWN

1 part vodka
1 part triple sec
1 part rum
1 part gin
1 part tequila
1 part sour mix
1 part blue curaçao

Shake with ice and strain into a shot glass.*

*Note: Because this recipe includes many ingredients,
it's easier to make in volume, about 6 shots.

WALTZING MATILDA

1 part light rum
1 part blue curaçao
1 part pineapple juice
Shake with ice and strain into a shot glass.

WAM BAS

1 part Southern Comfort®
1 part scotch
Layer in a shot glass.

WARM BLONDE

1 part Southern Comfort®
1 part amaretto
Layer in a shot glass.

WARM CARROT CAKE
1 part butterscotch schnapps
1 part cinnamon schnapps
1 part Irish cream
Shake with ice and strain into a shot glass.

WARM FUZZY
1 part peach schnapps
1 part blue curaçao
Shake with ice and strain into a shot glass.

WARM LEATHERETTE
2 parts amaretto
1 part grenadine
3 parts black sambuca
Layer in a shot glass.

WARM PUKE
1 part crème de banana
1 part Irish cream
1 part coconut liqueur
Layer in a shot glass.

WARP CORE BREACH
1 part Goldschläger®
1 part tequila
1 part whiskey
Shake with ice and strain into a shot glass.

WATER MOCCASIN
1 part Crown Royal® bourbon
1 part peach schnapps
1 part sweet and sour mix
Shake with ice and strain into a shot glass.

WATERFALL
1 part vodka
1 part melon liqueur
1 part fresh lime juice
Shake with ice and strain into a shot glass.

WATERLOO (SHOOTER)
1 part Mandarin Napoleon® liqueur
1 part spiced rum
1 part orange juice
Shake with ice and strain into a shot glass.

WATERMELON SHOOTER
1 part crème de noyaux
1 part amaretto
1 part pineapple juice
1 part Southern Comfort®
Shake with ice and strain into a shot glass.

WATERMELON SHOOTER (MODERN RECIPE)
1 part vodka
1 part melon liqueur
Shake with ice and strain into a shot glass.

WATERMELON SHOT
1 part vodka
1 part amaretto
1 part Southern Comfort®
Splash of orange juice
Shake with ice and strain into a shot glass.

WAYNE'S WORLD
1 part Jägermeister®
1 part sambuca
Shake with ice and strain into a shot glass.

WEASEL WATER
1 part cream
1 part crème de banana
Shake with ice and strain into a shot glass.

WEEK AT THE BEACH
1 part peach schnapps
1 part vodka
1 part orange juice
Shake with ice and strain into a shot glass.

WEEKEND ON THE BEACH
1 part blended scotch whiskey
1 part peach schnapps
1 part sweet and sour mix
1 part sour apple schnapps
Shake with ice and strain into a shot glass.

WELL-GREASED DWARF
1 part white crème de cacao
1 part sambuca
1 part Irish cream
Layer in a shot glass.

WENCH
1 part amaretto
1 part spiced rum
Shake with ice and strain into a shot glass.

WERTHERS
1 part Irish cream
1 part butterscotch schnapps
1 part Crown Royal® bourbon
Shake with ice and strain into a shot glass.

WEST SIDE SPECIAL
1 part Southern Comfort®
1 part peppermint schnapps
Shake with ice and strain into a shot glass.

WET BACK
1 part coffee liqueur
1 part tequila
Shake with ice and strain into a shot glass.

WET CROTCH
1 part triple sec
1 part Irish cream
1 part raspberry liqueur
Shake with ice and strain into a shot glass.

WET DREAM
1 part orange juice
1 part Galliano®
1 part triple sec
1 part club soda
Layer in a shot glass.

WET KISS
1 part amaretto
1 part sweet and sour mix
1 part watermelon schnapps
Layer in a shot glass.

WHAT CRISIS!
1 part peach schnapps
1 part melon liqueur
1 part orange juice
1 part cranberry juice cocktail
Shake with ice and strain into a shot glass.

WHIPSTER
1 part white crème de cacao
1 part apricot brandy
1 part triple sec
Layer in a shot glass.

WHISTLESTOP
1 part triple sec
1 part whiskey
Layer in a shot glass.

WHISTLING GYPSY
1 part coffee liqueur
1 part Irish cream
1 part Stolichnaya® vodka
Layer in a shot glass.

WHITE DEATH
1 part white crème de cacao
1 part vodka
1 part raspberry liqueur
Shake with ice and strain into a shot glass.

WHITE ELEPHANT (SHOOTER)
1 part vodka
1 part white crème de cacao
1 part cream
Shake with ice and strain into a shot glass.

WHITE KNUCKLE RIDE SHOOTER
1 part vodka
1 part coffee liqueur
Shake with ice and strain into a shot glass.

WHITE LIGHTNING
1 part tequila
1 part white crème de cacao
Layer in a shot glass.

WHITE MESS
1 part light rum
1 part crème de cassis
1 part root beer schnapps
1 part coconut rum
1 part heavy cream
Shake with ice and strain into a shot glass.*
*Note: Because this recipe includes many ingredients,
it's easier to make in volume, about 6 shots.

WHITE SATIN
1 part Tia Maria®
1 part cream
1 part Frangelico®
Shake with ice and strain into a shot glass.

WHITE SPIDER SHOOTER
1 part white crème de cacao
1 part vodka
Shake with ice and strain into a shot glass.

WHITE WOLF
1 part coffee liqueur
1 part Irish cream
1 part sambuca
Shake with ice and strain into a shot glass.

WHOOPASS

1 part triple sec
1 part vodka
1 part peach schnapps
1 part Key Largo® schnapps
1 part cranberry juice cocktail
1 part sweet and sour mix

Shake with ice and strain into a shot glass.*

*Note: Because this recipe contains many ingredients,
it's easier to make in volume, about 6 shots.

WICKED STEPMOTHER

1 part pepper-flavored vodka
1 part amaretto

Shake with ice and strain into a shot glass.

WIDE GLIDE

1 part peach schnapps
1 part dark rum

Shake with ice and strain into a shot glass.

WILD BERRY POP TART
1 part wild berry schnapps
1 part vodka
1 part strawberry liqueur
Shake with ice and strain into a shot glass.

WILD PEPPERTINI
1 part Wild Turkey®
1 part peppermint schnapps
Shake with ice and strain into a shot glass.

WILD SQUIRREL SEX
1 part lemon vodka
1 part strawberry vodka
1 part orange vodka
1 part raspberry vodka
1 part amaretto
Splash of sour mix
Splash of cranberry juice cocktail
Dash of grenadine
Shake with ice and strain into a shot glass.*
*Note: Because this recipe includes many ingredients,
it's easier to make in volume, about 6 shots.

WILL WILLY WANDER
1 part Southern Comfort®
1 part rock and rye
1 part crème de fraise
2 parts amaretto
Splash of sour mix
Splash of orange juice
Shake with ice and strain into a shot glass.*
*Note: Because this recipe includes many ingredients,
it's easier to make in volume, about 6 shots.

WILLY
1 part Southern Comfort®
1 part whiskey
1 part amaretto
1 part orange juice
Shake with ice and strain into a shot glass.

WINDEX (SHOOTER)
1 part blue curaçao
1 part vodka
Shake with ice and strain into a shot glass.

WINDSURFER
1 part coffee liqueur
1 part triple sec
1 part Yukon Jack®
Layer in a shot glass.

WINDY
1 part blue curaçao
1 part vodka
1 part pineapple juice
1 part sour mix
Layer in a shot glass.

WINTER BREAK
1 part peach schnapps
1 part banana liqueur
1 part Southern Comfort®
Layer in a shot glass.

WOMEN'S REVENGE
1 crème de menthe
1 part Irish cream
Shake with ice and strain into a shot glass.

WOO WOO SHOOTER
1 part peach schnapps
1 part vodka
1 part cranberry juice cocktail
Shake with ice and strain into a shot glass.

WOOF

1 part blue curaçao
1 part amaretto
1 part Marie Brissard Parfait Amour®
Shake with ice and strain into a shot glass.

WOO-SHOO

1 part cranberry vodka
1 part peach schnapps
Shake with ice and strain into a shot glass.

X

1 part amaretto
1 part wild berry schnapps
Splash of sour mix
Splash of cola
Shake with ice and strain into a shot glass.

YAK MILK
1 part dark crème de cacao
1 part coconut rum
Shake with ice and strain into a shot glass.

YAPS
1 part Yukon Jack®
1 part sour apple schnapps
Shake with ice and strain into a shot glass.

YELLOW BELLY COCKSUCKER
1 part orange-flavored vodka
1 part cinnamon schnapps
Shake with ice and strain into a shot glass.

YELLOW SNOW
1 part vodka
1 part pineapple juice
Shake with ice and strain into a shot glass.

YELLOW WORM
1 part tequila blanco
1 part crème de banana
Shake with ice and strain into a shot glass.

YIN YANG
1 part Jägermeister®
1 part 100-proof peppermint schnapps
Shake with ice and strain into a shot glass.

YOOHA
1 part whiskey
1 part Yoo-Hoo Chocolate Drink®
Shake with ice and strain into shot glass.

YOU DRIVEA ME CRAZY
1 part pineapple juice
1 part 151-proof rum
1 part coconut rum
Dash of grenadine
Shake with ice and strain into a shot glass.

YUKON CORNELIUS
1 part Yukon Jack®
1 part Goldschläger®
Shake with ice and strain into a shot glass.

Z STREET SLAMMER
1 part crème de banana
1 part pineapple juice
1 part grenadine
Shake with ice and strain into a shot glass.

Z-28
1 part crème de menthe
1 part banana liqueur
1 part tequila
Layer in a shot glass.

ZENMEISTER
1 part Jägermeister®
1 part root beer
Shake with ice and strain into a shot glass.

ZIPPER
1 part triple sec
1 part tequila
1 part Irish cream
Layer in a shot glass.

ZOO STATION
1 part amaretto
1 part coffee liqueur
1 part Irish cream
1 part banana liqueur
1 part cream
Shake with ice and strain into a shot glass.*

*Note: Because this recipe includes many ingredients,
it's easier to make in volume, about 6 shots.*

ZOOT SUIT RIOT
1 part apricot brandy
1 part blackberry liqueur
1 part cranberry juice cocktail
1 part Southern Comfort®
Shake with ice and strain into a shot glass.

ZOWIE
1 part banana liqueur
1 part Irish cream
1 part coconut rum
Layer in a shot glass.

ZUC
1 part crème de menthe
1 part coffee liqueur
1 part Irish cream
1 part triple sec
Layer in a shot glass.

BONUS SHOTS

10-LB SLEDGEHAMMER

1 part tequila
1 part whiskey
Pour ingredients into a glass neat
(do not chill).

19 DUKE DRIVE

1 part chocolate mint liqueur
1 part cherry brandy
1 part crème de banana
Layer in a shot glass.

24K NIGHTMARE
1 part Goldschläger®
1 part Jägermeister®
1 part 100-proof peppermint schnapps
1 part 151-proof rum
Shake with ice and strain into a shot glass.

252
1 part 151-proof rum
1 part bourbon
Shake with ice and strain into a shot glass.

401
1 part Irish cream
1 part crème de banana
1 part coffee liqueur
1 part Yukon Jack®
Layer in a shot glass.

44D

1 part peach schnapps
1 part coffee liqueur
1 part vodka
Splash of grenadine
Shake first three ingredients with ice and
strain into a shot glass.
Top the glass with grenadine.

49ER GOLD RUSH

1 part Goldschläger®
1 part tequila
Shake with ice and strain into a shot glass.

50-50 BAR
1 part Irish cream
1 part coffee liqueur
Splash of 151-proof rum
Shake first two ingredients with ice and
strain into a shot glass.
Top the glass with the rum.

'57 CHEVY
1 part Southern Comfort®
1 part triple sec
1 part amaretto
Splash of orange juice
Splash of pineapple juice
Splash of grenadine
Splash of lemon lime soda
Shake with ice and strain into a shot glass.*
Note: Because this recipe includes many ingredients,
it's easier to make in volume, about 6 shots.

69ER IN A POOL
1 part vodka
1 part 151-proof rum
Dash of lemon juice
Drop of hot sauce
Layer in a shot glass.

77J 1
1 part rum cream liqueur
1 part amaretto
1 part coffee liqueur
Layer in a shot glass.

77J 2
1 part vodka
1 part coconut liqueur
Shake with ice and strain into a shot glass.

141

1 part Irish cream
1 part amaretto
1 part coffee liqueur
Shake with ice and strain into a shot glass.

8 IRON

1 part blue curaçao
1 part ouzo
1 part banana liqueur
Shake with ice and strain into a shot glass.

911

1 part 100-proof peppermint schnapps
1 part 100-proof cinnamon schnapps
Dash of hot sauce
Pour ingredients into a glass neat
(do not chill).

INDEX

Sunrise, 337; Irish Sunset, 337; Irish Tricolour, 338; Irish Widow, 338; Jager Oatmeal Cookie, 345; Jamaica 10 Speed, 347; Jedi Mind Probe, 349; Jelly Fish, 353; Killer Oreos, 362; Kilted Black Leprechaun, 363; Kiss of Death, 363; Klondike, 363; The Kooch, 366; Land Rover, 370; Landslide #2, 371; Lava Lamp, 373; Leather and Lace #2, 375; Leprechaun's Gold, 378; Lewinsky, 379; Licorice Heart, 380; Liquid Quaalude, 389; Lit City, 389; Lube Job, 395; Mad Scientist, 399; Martian Hard-on, 402; McTavish, 403; Mexican Breeze, 407; Milk of Amnesia, 412; Milky Way #2, 412; Milky Way #3, 413; Mint Chocolate, 415; Monkey's Punch, 417; Moose Fart, 418; Mud Slide, 421; Mushroom, 421; Mutated Mother's Milk, 422; Napalm-Death, 424; Nipple on Fire, 429; Nuts 'n Holly, 433; Nuts 'n Nipples, 433; Nutty Irishman, 434; Nutty Professor #1, 435; Oatmeal Cookie #1, 437; Oatmeal Cookie #2, 438; Oatmeal Cookie #3, 438; Oatmeal Cookie #4, 438; Oatmeal Raisin Cookie, 439; Open Grave, 443; Oreo Cookie, 445; Orgasm, 445; P.D.C., 456; Pearl Necklace, 459; Pierced Buttery Nipple, 463; Pierced Nipple. 464; Pineapple Upside-down Cake, 465; Pink Belly, 466; P.M.F., 471; Poison Milk, 473; P.S. I Love You, 477; Pumpkin Pie, 479; Puppy's Nose, 479; Rabbit Punch, 487; Raider, 488; Rattlesnake, 491; Rattlesnake Shooter, 491; El Revolto, 500; Rock Lobster #1, 503; Rugmuncher, 510; Runny Nose, 511; Sandy Beach, 519; Scooby Snack #2, 522; Screaming Moose, 525; Screaming Orgasm Shooter, 525; Scurvy, 526; Seduction, 527; Shamrock Shooter, 534; Silly Surfer, 550; Silver Thread, 542; Sit on My Face, Mary Jane, 543; Sit on My Face, Sammy, 544; Skull, 544; Slippery Nipple, 547; Smashing Pumpkin, 550; Snapshot, 555; Snow Cap, 557; Spice Cake, 570; Spicy Buttery Nipple, 572; Squished Smurf, 573; SR-71, 574; Stained Blue Dress, 575; Stevie Ray Vaughn, 576; Stiff Dick, 577; Storm, 579; Storm Cloud, 580; Storm Warning, 580; Strawberry Kiss, 582; Streetcar, 582; Stroke, 583; Summer Fling, 585; Swamp Thing, 588; Swiss Hiker, 592; Swiss and Whoosh, 592; Take Me Away, 594; Tasty Orgasm, 595; Test Tube Baby, 598; Tetanus Shot, 599; The Texas Mud Slide, 599; To the Moon, 607; Toolkit, 608; Under Water, 617; V-2 Schnieder, 621; Varicose Veins, 622;

After Eight, 329; Iguana, 329; Illusion, 330; Immaculate Ingestion, 331; International Incident, 332; Italian Russian, 339; Italian Valium, 341; Jamaican Bobsled, 347; Jamboree, 349; Cape Cods, 350; Lemonheads, 350; Johnny on the Beach, 355; Jolly Rancher #2, 356; Juicy Lips, 358; Kamikaze, 360; Key West Shooter, 361; Kiwiki, 364; Komy Shot, 365; Kool-Aid, 366; Kool-Aid Shot, 367; Kremlin Shooter, 367; Lemon Meringue, 376; Lime Lizard, 382; Lime-Light, 382; Liquid Candy Cane #1, 383; Liquid Cocaine, #1, 384; Liquid Cocaine, #3, 385; Liquid Cocaine, #4, 385; Liquid Heroin, 388; A Little Nervous, 391; Lube Job, 395; Lui Lui, 395; Mad Hatter, 398; Mad Melon Shooter, 398; Mage's Fire, 399; Maggots, 400; Manchurian Candidate, 401; Melon Ball, 405; Meloncholy Baby, 405; Melonoma, 406; Memory Loss, 406; Mild Jizz, 411; Mind Eraser, 414; Moose Fart, 418; Morning Wood, 419; Mother Load, 419; Mother Pucker, 420; Mouthwash, 420; Mud Slide, 421; Naked Navel, 423; Neon Bullfrog, 426; Nero's Delight, 427; Neuronium, 427; Nuclear Waste, 431; Nut-Cracker, 432; Nuthugger, 433; Oatmeal Raisin Cookie, 439; Opera House Special, 443; Orange Crush Shooter, 444; Oreo Cookie, 445; Orgies with a Cherry, 445; Pair o' Cakes, 449; Pants on Fire, 450; Paralyzer, 452; PB&J #1, 455; Peach Nehi, 456; Peach Tart #2, 458; Pee Gee, 460; Photon Torpedo, 463; Pigskin Shot, 464; Pineapple Upside-down Cake, 465; Pink Cadillac, 467; Pink Floyd, 467; Pink Lemonade Shooter, 468; Pipeline, 469; Pleading Insanity, 470; Poco Loco Boom, 471; Poison Apple, 472; The Polish Pounder, 473; Porto Covo, 475; Power Drill, 475; Power Shot, 475; Purple Elastic Thunder Fuck, 481; Purple Hooter, 482; Purple Rain, 483; Purple Viper, 483; Pussy Juice, 485; Pyro, 485; Raspberry Tootsie Roll Pop, 490; Red Death, 495; Red Square, 497; Red-Eyed Hell, 498; Red-Eyed Shooter, 498; Rich, Creamy Butter, 501; Rocket Fuel #2, 504; Rocky Mountain Butter-fly, 505; Rosso di Sera, 507; Rot Gut, 507; Ruby Red, 510; Rumka, 511; Russian Apple, 511; Russian Ballet, 512; Russian Bloody Mary, 512; Russian Candy, 512; Russian Defect, 513; Russian Quaalude, 513; Russian Roulette, 513; Russian Shamrock, 514; Sambuca Slide, 516; Sand Slide, 518; Scorpion Shooter, 522; Screamer, 523;